Twenty Years of
Poem of the Week.com

Twenty Years of Poem of the Week.com

edited by
Andrew McFadyen-Ketchum

LAKE DALLAS, TEXAS

FIRST EDITION

Requests for permission to reprint or reuse
material from this work should be sent to:

Permissions
Madville Publishing
PO Box 358
Lake Dallas, TX 75065

Cover Design: Jacqueline V. Davis
Editor Photo: Karen Carr

ISBN: 978-1-963695-59-5 Paper, 978-1-963695-60-1 ebook
Library of Congress Control Number: 2025945997

Contents

xi   *Andrew McFadyen-Ketchum*
PREFACE

xiv   *Brian Brodeur*
FEELING AND KNOWING—INTRODUCTION

1   *Dilruba Ahmed*
GHAZAL

2   *Dan Albergotti*
NEITHER

4   *Rick Barot*
TWO VIDEO INSTALLATIONS

6   *Dawn Pichón Barron*
MAN CAMPS

7   *Zeina Hashem Beck*
MESSAGE FROM MY AUNT ON HER SON'S DEATH ANNIVERSARY

8   *Sheila Black*
RADIUM DREAM

9   *Kimberly M. Blaeser*
THIS STRANGER'S BEAUTY

10   *Tommye Blount*
AMERICANA ELEGY

11   *Kristin Bock*
THE DREAMING RIFLE

17   *Dexter L. Booth*
CONVERSATION STARTERS OR THINGS I'D NEVER SAY TO YOU IN
    PUBLIC

19   *Sara Borjas*
POCHA CAFÉ

22   *Mark J. Brewin*
BURNING DOWN THE CAMPER

24   *Bill Brown*
ELEMENTAL

26   *Derrick Weston Brown*
THE ROOT, A HAIBUN FOR D'ANGELO

29   *Nickole Brown*
A PRAYER TO TALK TO ANIMALS

31   *J. Scott Brownlee*
INTO THE VALLEY OAK THAT WILL NOT SING, THAT WILL NOT
    EVEN TALK

33   *Lauren Camp*
     TO FAIL AND FAIL AND STILL GO ON

35   *Marci Calabretta Cancio-Bello*
     RESTITUTION FOR THE GRANDSON

37   *Kara Candito*
     A SHORT GENEALOGY OF POWER TOOLS

38   *Cyrus Cassells*
     THE SHADOW

40   *Jennifer Chang*
     THE WINTER'S WIFE

41   *Grant Clauser*
     LUCKY

43   *Kai Coggin*
     THE FIRST KISS I DON'T COUNT

46   *Aaron Coleman*
     VESTIGIA

47   *Nicole Cooley*
     ROMANCE

49   *Steve Davenport*
     ARRANGE THEIR SEA-SMOOTH BONES IN FOURTEEN BROKEN
          ROWS

50   *Todd Davis*
     LAST OF DECEMBER

51   *Linda Bryant Davis*
     DIGEST OF RED

53   *Tyree Daye*
     LORD HERE

54   *Linh Dinh*
     BORDERLESS BODY

56   *Camille Dungy*
     A MASSIVE DYING OFF

59   *Martín Espada*
     FLOATERS

62   *Blas Falconer*
     A LOVE POEM

64   *Nick Flynn*
     BAG OF MICE

65   *CMarie Fuhrman*
     CAMPED BENEATH THE DAM

67   *Ross Gay*
     NURSERY

69 *Hollay Ghadery*
    REBELLION BOX

71 *Aracelis Girmay*
    THE BLACK MARIA

75 *Eugene Gloria*
    SAINT JOE

77 *Laurie Ann Guerrero*
    ON EATING RATTLESNAKE

78 *Tami Haaland*
    DEER ON CRAZY CREEK

79 *Forrest Hamer*
    UNCLE

80 *Sam Hamill*
    THE ORCHID FLOWER

82 *Jeff Hardin*
    FROM HERE TO THERE

83 *Gustavo Hernandez*
    WINTER CUMBIA WITH BROTHER AND SISTER

84 *Lee Herrick*
    FLIGHT

86 *Ishmael Angaluuk Hope*
    ARRANGEMENTS

87 *LeAnne Howe*
    MY NAME IS NOBLE SAVAGE

89 *TR Hummer*
    CORROSIVE LYRIC

90 *Major Jackson*
    LEAVING SATURN—SUN RA & HIS YEAR 2000 MYTH SCIENCE
        ARKESTRAAT GRENDEL'S LAIR CABARET, 1986

92 *Jessica Jacobs*
    PRIMER

93 *Luke Johnson*
    BEE FENNEL

94 *Judy Jordan*
    AFTER THE FARMER'S MARKET

100 *Allison Joseph*
    THE WORLD'S WORST JUKEBOX

102 *Brigit Pegeen Kelly*
    THE DRAGON

104 *Suji Kwock Kim*
    GENERATION

108 *James Kimbrell*
MT. PISGAH

109 *Christine Kitano*
SKY COUNTRY

112 *Ruth Ellen Kocher*
COSMOGONY

114 *Jason Koo*
BEGIN, BEING, BEGIN

118 *Ed Bok Lee*
MITOCHONDRIAL EVENING

123 *Mari L'Esperance*
SOMETHING COMING APART

125 *Raina León*
BANNED PORTRAIT IN THE MAGA ERA: STUDY SAYS BLACK
GIRLS ARE "LESS INNOCENT"

127 *Hugh Martin*
M16A2 ASSAULT RIFLE

128 *David Tomas Martinez*
TATTLETALE

130 *Khaled Mattawa*
MALOUK'S QASSIDA

131 *Donovan McAbee*
MAMA'S BODY

136 *Nathan McClain*
"FIRE DESTROYS BELOVED CHICAGO BAKERY"

138 *Campbell McGrath*
PICASSO (1937)

141 *Shivani Mehta*
THE MUSEUM

142 *Wayne Miller*
A PRAYER (O CITY—)

145 *Deborah A. Miranda*
HOW TO LOVE THE BURNING WORLD

147 *Juan J. Morales*
A GOOD EDUCATION

148 *John Murillo*
DISTANT LOVER (OR, WHEN YOU'RE TEACHING IN AMHERST
AND, WHILE ON A LATE NIGHT WALK, YOUR WIFE CALLS
FROM BROOKLYN TO SAY GOODNIGHT)

149 *Frank Paino*
ROUGH ALCHEMY

151 *Gregory Pardlo*

WINTER AFTER THE STRIKE

154 *Ed Pavlic*
MASQUALÉRO

157 *Monica Prince*
THREE SCENES FROM *ROADMAP: A CHOREOPOEM*

163 *Octavio Quintanilla*
SONNET FOR HUMAN SMUGGLERS

164 *Saara Myrene Raapana*
SMOKE

166 *Khalisa Rae*
MAD. BLACK. BIRD.

168 *Paisley Rekdal*
WHY SOME GIRLS LOVE HORSES

170 *Gerard Robledo*
THE LAST DAYS OF SUMMER

173 *Steve Scafidi*
ON THE OCCASION OF AN ARGUMENT BESIDE THE RIVER
    WHERE I LIVE

175 *Tim Seibles*
TRYING FOR FIRE

179 *Said Shaiye*
A FELA KUTI STORY

183 *Enid Shomer*
DRIVING THROUGH THE ANIMAL

185 *ire'ne lara silva*
IN MY HEART

187 *Leah Silvieus*
MATTHEW 19:14

189 *ML Smoker*
TATOGANA

190 *Angela Narciso Torres*
THINGS TO TELL MY SON ABOUT THE MOON

191 *Brian Turner*
CURFEW

192 *Connie Voisine*
THE EARLY DAYS OF AVIATION

195 *Mark Wagenaar*
CHIROPRACTIC (BOOTBLACKS & LIGHT BULBS)

197 *Michael Walsh*
THE GHOST STORY THEY TELL ABOUT YOU

199 *Sarah Rebecca Warren*
CHIMAYÓ MILAGROS

200 *L. Lamar Wilson*
TIMES LIKE THESE: MARIANNA, FLORIDA

201 *Jennifer Yáñez-Alaniz*
PATRON SAINT OF MOIST THINGS

202 *Matthew Yeager*
A BIG BALL OF FOIL IN A SMALL NY APARTMENT

206 *Jake Adam York*
DARKLY

210 *Acknowledgments*
215 *About the Editor*

PREFACE

PoemoftheWeek.com is an act of sharing. Of giving. Of gratitude. Wrapped all into one. Much like the 1,500+ poems that make it, and the 100 poems that compose this anthology, 20 years in the making. No matter what a poem says or who wrote it or in what ways it fails and succeeds, a poem is always an act of sharing, of giving, of gratitude.

I was feeling all the above when I founded PoemoftheWeek.com in the Fall of 2006. I was in my first semester of graduate school at Southern Illinois University Carbondale. In my first poetry workshop, Professor Judy Jordan handed out a hand-scrawled list of 100 or so books she expected us to have read by the end of term. So I got to work and by week four, my mind was swirling with a poetry I didn't know existed: living poets writing living words that leapt off the page and seeped their way in. I dreamt poetry. Writing it. Reading it. Meeting the poets who had somehow written the poems that astonished me so. I discovered that more than anything, I wanted to share. I wanted to find a way to give all this startling verse to friends and family like gifts. I wanted to express my gratitude for the poems that were teaching me how to write my own. I wanted to express gratitude for poetry itself.

The idea was simple: Email a listserv of friends, colleagues, and family each week with a poem from one of the books I'd read for class. My first selection was "Mt. Pisgah" from James Kimbrell's masterful *The Gatehouse Heaven*. "Mt. Pisgah" woo'd me with its sonnet-like structure, how it managed in sixteen lines to open a complex world of water and snakes and silence and moons, all in a local language just about anyone could enjoy. I sent off that first celebration email and never looked back.

That listserv quickly turned into PoemoftheWeek.org in 2007. Back in those days, the debate between web and print was only just brewing. Very few journals were online. Few literary publications or institutions resembling POW existed.

For the first ten years of POW's existence, I hand-selected every single weekly celebration and interviewed the poets about their process, lives, and work. Twenty snippets of these interviews appear throughout the anthology. While this method proved fantastically effective (by year ten, POW had amassed over ten million hits), I felt the website needed an evolving aesthetic—fresh eyes with a fresh vision of what a great poem could be.

For the tenth anniversary of POW in 2016, I redesigned the website, switched over to the .com, and started employing the assistance of guest editors, including:

Phillip B Williams, Fall 2016
Mark J Brewin, Spring 2016
TR Hummer, Fall 2017
Judy Jordan, Spring 2017
Tyree Daye, Fall 2018
Ocean Vuong, Spring 2018
Vandana Khanna, Spring 2019
Luke Johnson, Spring 2020
Angela Narciso Torres, Fall 2020
Cyrus Cassells, Spring 2021
CMarie Fuhrman, Fall 2021 & Spring 2022
Michael Walsh, Fall 2022
Gerard Robledo, Spring 2023
Karen Carr, Fall 2023
Sheila Black, Spring 2024
Hollay Ghadery, Fall 2024
& Lee Herrick, Spring 2025

I am ever so thankful for their assistance in selecting celebrations for the past ten years and for their service to the poetry community itself. It's no easy task to select 16 poets off one's bookshelf to celebrate when there are so many poets to love.

Which brings us to today, another ten years later, 20 years after that first celebration. How to select 100 poems from the 1500+ on the archive? You read. And read. And read some more. You come up with rubrics to determine the greatness of a poem that would make Dr. J. Evans Pritchard cringe. You print out every poem you ever celebrated, throw them up in the air at the park, and snag 100 poems as they fall out of the sky. You come up with lists you then delete. Anything to get to re-know the work you have created until the subconscious starts speaking names and you write them down.

The result of that process is now in your hands. *Twenty Years of PoemoftheWeek. com* represents some of the best North American poetry published since 2000 and is the first truly comprehensive anthology of 21st Century North American verse. Unfolding in real time and chosen by a diverse selection of accomplished editor-poets, the 100 poems enclosed aren't just poems I love or ones POW's guest editors love; they are poems that speak to the community and the times we share. Ultimately, *Twenty Years of PoemoftheWeek.com* is a communal act all poets and lovers of verse can claim and gift as their own.

It is my great hope that you will read this book and feel it is yours. To read again and again. To loan to friends. To assign in your classrooms. There is a poetry here that can speak to us all—the large and the small parts. Indigenous poets will be found here. Queer poets. Black poets. Poets with disabilities/ disabled poets. Poets you have known all your life alongside poets you'll have to google. Each page, I pray is a delight. I hope these verses bring you to tears. If they make you angry, write a poem you didn't know you had in you. No matter what your poem says or who you are as you write it or how it succeeds or fails, be sure it is an act of sharing, of giving, of gratitude.

—Andrew McFadyen-Ketchum
February 14, 2026, Nashville, Tennessee

Brian Brodeur
FEELING AND KNOWING—INTRODUCTION

In a 1938 essay on the logical deficiencies of Shakespeare's sonnets, John Crowe Ransom distinguished between a poetry of knowledge and a poetry of feeling. Ransom observed a general preference since the Romantic period for the latter, the principle objective of which is emotive expression. According to Ransom, the poetry of feeling "taints us with subjectivism, sentimentality, and self-indulgence." Rather than argument and elaboration, irony and paradox, or thought and feeling braided into one spiraling conceit, such poems lean too hard on hermetic impulses and stylistic quirks. Such poetry beguiles and diverts the reader, who receives the spectacle of the poem as a passive observer, like a live studio audience prompted by blinking signs to laugh, clap, gasp, boo, or cry.

During the intervening ninety years since Ransom's essay, little has changed in this regard. As with Shakespeare's sonnets, what saves the poetry of feeling is an exacting sense of form, which persuades readers, as Ransom observed, "that this is a poetry of precision, when logically it is a poetry of wonderful imprecision." Precise form coupled with the irregularity of authorial whims and peculiar attitudes can pressurize a poem. Measure objectifies, rendering even a passing thought durable. Byron's "Pleasure's a sin, and sometimes sin's a pleasure," for example, achieves memorability through its chiasmic syntax and pentametric line, as well as the statement's function as a cheeky aside within the larger mock-heroic structure of *Don Juan*.

Now that modernism, postmodernism, and metamodernism have relegated meter and rhyme to the dusty attic of poesy's archaisms, this craft or sullen art has become subjective to the point of eccentricity—a predicament worsened by poetry's abdication of narrative, drama, satire, didacticism, and exposition to other genres, media, and modes. Readers both casual and professional take for granted that a principle function of poetry—perhaps its only function—is self-expression. Poetry *feels* more than it *thinks*, emoting instead of knowing. In fact, uncertainty (*not* knowing) has become compulsory in contemporary poetry. This has had a narrowing effect, limiting poetry's power to embody, as Elizabeth Bishop wrote in praise of baroque prose, "not a thought, but a mind thinking."

What contemporary poetry knows most is that it doesn't know. Good poets acknowledge this truism without squatting on it like a golden egg. Thankfully, *Twenty Years of Poem of the Week* includes many poets who don't default to feeling as a mode du jour. Nor do these poets stiffen into cold intellectualization. Addressing contemporary concerns, many poets utilize various traditions ranging from Japanese tanka and medieval bestiary to more or less ubiquitous forms like the ghazal, sestina, and prose poem. The tradition that poets in this anthology rely on most is the sonnet—that lyric nexus of argument and song that encourages the unification of thought and feeling within a compressed poetic space.

Here's a compelling example by Octavio Quintanilla:

SONNET FOR HUMAN SMUGGLERS

Take care of them. If they want water,
        Dump them in the river. If they crave
Freedom, let them loose among rattlesnakes.
        If they want to breathe, let them breathe dust.

Let the desert mouse nest in their white bones.
Give them shelter with your greed. With your rape.

The roadkill is a sign you're almost home.
        Point to it and show them who they are.
Their life's a documentary, a newscast.

        But for you, everything is possible.
You're the map that leads them astray,
        Priest leading a funeral procession.

Load this cargo. Shackle them with promises,
        Backaches that keep them from killing you.

The poem begins by punning on the phrase "take care," a cartoony gangster euphemism for "kill." Unlike many contemporary sonnets less concerned with meeting the challenges inherent within the form, Quintanilla develops a violent and ironic conceit reminiscent of Donne's "Batter my heart, three-person'd God." Quintanilla, with his image of the "map that leads them astray," also alludes to a trope favored by another famous sonneteer, Robert Frost, whose narrator/guide in "Directive" "only has at heart your getting lost." Though readers may lament the absence of meter and rhyme in Quintanilla's poem, one soon appreciates the map-less disorientation that this omission brings to the conceit.

At first, Quintanilla's poem appears to address the smugglers, who the poet compares to a "Priest leading a funeral procession" of innumerable migrant bodies brutally likened to "roadkill." With ambiguity further reminiscent of Frost, Quintanilla invites and/or orders the smugglers to point out animal corpses along the road not to show the migrants what they are or what they will become but as a way of revealing the smuggler's inhumanity. The poet asserts in unvarying iambic pentameter in his only regularly metrical line, "The roadkill is a sign you're almost home," which suggests a final resting place for the perpetrators, a gesture whereby Quintanilla, as ironic guide to the guides, concedes his own violent intensions.

The poet further signals these intentions through the preposition in the poem's title. Because Quintanilla apostrophizes the smugglers, the reader might expect the title to be "Sonnet to Human Smugglers." Quintanilla's "for," however, recasts the poem as a revenge fantasy, suggesting the possibility that the poem's "you" is actually the migrants who the poet advises to "take care" of the smugglers. As with Donne's ironic appeal to God to renew him by breaking him, Quintanilla manages to have his argument both ways.

To avoid falsely classifying the primary mode of this anthology as traditional or formal, I should interject that these one-hundred contemporary poems are almost entirely composed in unrhymed free-verse—the default method in the United States since Imagism crossed the Atlantic over a century ago. This aspect of the anthology is representative of broader trends, though it ignores an exciting turn to meter and rhyme by younger poets such as Chad Abushanab, Morri Creech, Amit Majmudar, Shane McCrae, Alexis Sears, A. E. Stallings, Caki Wilkinson, and others.

The technical facility of the poets in this anthology ranges from adequate to excellent, as in these lines that either approximate or reproduce iambic pentameter: "The women of the village wept when your father died" (from Camille Dungy's "A Massive Dying Off"); "It will be years before I understand" (from Jennifer Chang's "The Winter's Wife"); "A Florida child knows the safest part" (from Jessica Jacobs's "Primer"); and "Why so much hoodoo about heaven / when the river and this life demand our praise" (from Bill Brown's "Elemental"). Such lines exemplify a taut application of free verse illustrative of the finest work being published today. The free verse represented in this anthology includes the usual varieties: parsing meter, grammatical parallelism, metrical similitude, open-field composition, Psalm-like runover lines, and even the occasional passage or entire poem in accentual or syllabic verse. Even if the reader can't identify a specific formal principle, discerning in that the rhythms of each line accrue into a measured cadence distinctive from that of prose is apparent to a wakened attention.

Many of the poets in this anthology write within traditions that diverge from those of canonical English-language poetry (white, male)—a crosscurrent that has become a convention of its own. (We might pause here to remember that the idea of the canon originated with early Christian theologians choosing which texts to include as biblical "truths" and which to exclude because they diverged from the emergent orthodoxy, thus creating the cognate idea of extra- or anti-canonical texts such as the Gnostic gospels.)

One of the most exciting of the so-called anti-canon poets in the anthology is Sara Borjas, who identifies as "a Xicanx pocha." Borjas's poem "Pocha Café" presents a rollicky dramatic monologue spoken by a collective "we" restauranteur to a collective "you" clientele. Both "we" and "you," however, belong to the same community: "pochas," a derogatory term that Borjas defined in a recent Zoom-reading video as "white-washed Mexicans," Xicanx perceived by native-born Mexicans to have forgotten or rejected their heritage.

"Pocha Café" opens by establishing a tripartite we-you-them structure that evokes the dizzying sense of displacement shared by those who the poet invites to repurpose this pejorative as a term of identity whereby they might embrace cultural cliches:

> At Pocha Café, we play
> *Blood in Blood Out* and *Stand and Deliver* and mistake
> someone's dad on the daily for Edward James Olmos.
> Even we think all Mexicans look alike, or that all Latinos
>
> are Mexican and that's why our Salvadorian
> and Boricua homies talk shit but that's what people do
> when they love you so fuck it! If you are a downright
> cultural traitor, come on in! Here, at Pocha Café
>
> we only order rice and don't speak Spanish so we
> don't get corrected and we *stay out the fuckin kitchen*
> like our mamas told us and we refuse lemons
> and corridos in solidarity.

Borjas flourishes in contradictions. Appropriating the convention of the marketing pitch for the anti-capitalist project of lyric poetry, she utilizes a tone of inclusivity to build an exclusive, if fantastical space in which only a single marginalized group is welcome. Out of place in both Mexican and white US-American contexts, the collective narrator encourages a "pocha" multitude, with its cultural "impurities," to celebrate, as it were, their inauthentic authenticity.

For all Borjas's postcolonial rhetoric ("You ain't about colonizing the self, you're about / decolonizing your consciousness"), she utilizes one of the oldest dramatic conventions in Western literature: the Sophoclean chorus. This apparent contradiction only strengthens her argument that this democratically "broken" subculture represents a distinctly American grab-bag phenomenon in which anything can be assimilated: "Enjoy a quesadilla with American cheese!" Rather than representing dominant cultural values, like the Theban citizenry of *Antigone*, the chorus of Borjas's poem encourages "pochas" not to force themselves to squeeze into any prevailing hegemony, but to remain perpetually separate. Only through this separateness will they achieve distinction. "Come be / the part of yourself that scares the entire family!" Borjas implores with campy wit. Such imperatives to be "part," incorrect, and "befuddled half-ass" lead the reader to shrug with delicious exasperation, asking: "'Solidarity' to *what*?"

By way of contrast, I'd like to praise one of the more conventional poems in the anthology: Brigit Pegeen Kelly's dark fable "The Dragon." This lyric-narrative recounts a kind of Edenic pastoral dream-vision reminiscent of similar poems like Andrew Marvell's "The Garden" and Anthony Hecht's "A Hill." Kelly's poem begins:

> The bees came out of the junipers, two small swarms
> The size of melons; and golden, too, like melons,
> They hung next to each other, at the height of a deer's breast
> Above the wet black compost. And because
> The light was very bright it was hard to see them,
> And harder still to see what hung between them.
> A snake hung between them. The bees held up a snake,
> Lifting each side of his narrow neck, just below
> The pointed head, and in this way, very slowly
> They carried the snake through the garden

More quixotic anecdote than fully enumerated narrative (Does a snake have a "neck"?), Kelly's poem takes a hackneyed allegory and makes it strange by further mythologizing the figures of snake, Eve, garden, and God. Despite

Kelly's sober tone, she plays with and plays up these figures, accentuating latter-day exegeses:

> I kept thinking the snake
> Might be a hose, held by two ghostly hands,
> But the snake was a snake, his body green as the grass,
> His tail divided, his skin oiled the way the male member
> Is oiled by the female's juices

By sexualizing the snake, Kelly demystifies it. But, ironically, through her debunking of biblical analogues (her rendering of the garden as "Ungodly"), she exposes the inherent, irreligious mysteries therein—the symbolic correspondences latent within nature as well as the human impulse to order the world into symbols. In this regard, Kelly views the nature as a wilderness of hermeneutic archetypes constantly mediated by human logos, which prevents us from perceiving external reality as it truly is, free from human interpretation.

Another poem in the anthology similarly troubled by symbology is Nick Flynn's provocative "Bag of Mice." Though composed almost entirely of menacing images, the poem displays a compelling hypnogogic logic, turning at exactly the place a sonnet would in the ninth line:

BAG OF MICE

> I dreamt your suicide note
> was scrawled in pencil on a brown paperbag,
> & in the bag were six baby mice. The bag
> opened into darkness,
> smoldering
> from the top down. The mice,
> huddled at the bottom, scurried the bag
>> across a shorn field. I stood over it
>> & as the burning reached each carbon letter
>> of what you'd written
>> your voice released into the night
>> like a song, & the mice
>> grew wilder.

No doubt informed by American surrealist poets like Russell Edson, Charles Simic, and James Tate, Flynn's poem—bizarre as it first appears—employs a clear narrative line. A Jungian therapist's paraphrase of the plot might read: *A paper bag on which the suicide note of the analysand's mother has been written contains six mice pups that he refers to as "baby." The bag, "smoldering," slowly burns down, threatening the pups, who, through their panicked scurrying to escape, transport the bag across a stubble field. Their attempt to flee, however, only hastens their demise. As the bag burns, the writing disappears, transubstantiating the text into the literal "voice" of the deceased, which causes the mice to grow "wilder." Note: Analysand is a lyric poet (preoccupied by "song") and, since the mother's suicide, has struggled with addiction ("grew wilder") and depression ("darkness").*

Strange as these elements are, more unsettling is the narrator's emotional remove not only from the nightmarish scene but from the poem's lyric "you." The factual presentation and dryly descriptive tone galvanize the unsettling subject (a burning bag of mice) and tragic topic (a mother's suicide). That same analyst might emphasize the triple threat that the mice pups face. First, they've been unnaturally deprived of their mother—a circumstance that would likely lead to their death. Second, they've been placed within the suffocating and dangerous "night" of the suicide's aftermath. Third, the mice face the further threat of the mother's "smoldering" and disembodied voice that sings what must sound like a feeble song—an insufficient explanation for her own absence.

This leaves Flynn's poem burning like an atavistic vision that summons the reader to its dim light. Standing helpless over the mice, neither poet nor reader can intervene.

Another fantastical narrative that thinks its way through a coiled agglomeration of ideas and images is Matthew Yeager's "A Big Ball of Foil in a Small NY Apartment." This parabolic *ars poetica* tells the story of a man who decides to save every sheet of aluminum foil he finds, adding these to a wadded ball that soon becomes an "awesome and beautiful" art object:

> As the months went by, the ball grew. It grew and grew.
> It grew until it had to be moved from the oven,
> where he'd kept it to save space, into the open, onto the floor.
> It grew till it couldn't fit through the window or door.
> It grew until furniture had to be moved, first
> to new places in his apartment, then out onto the street.

Here, art displaces life—the act of making becomes an obsession too imposing to control. The specific poesis that the protagonist undertakes repurposes utilitarian objects into an aesthetic context, in much the same way that the poet recovers the found object of language and transforms it into art. Rather than a *homo symbolicum* manipulating signs to imitate external reality, Yeager's foil artist seems sandwiched, if you will, between two theories of representation: expressionism and formalism. Though the protagonist's magnum opus is abstract (a "ball" that can't be played with), it still represents the essence of the artist's intensions, even if these remain mysterious to him.

This becomes the poem's essential conflict: For whom or what does the artist make art? In Yeager's terms, the protagonist recontextualizes "trash" into "treasure." But this treasure only has value or meaning to the maker (who doesn't necessarily know what or how it means). In other words, the "ball" becomes a foil against the protagonist's original impulse to create art "as he wished it to be." Inevitably, the art object, if it is to have any lasting value, must supersede the intentions of the artist. No surprise in the maker, no surprise in the viewer.

Yeager's decision to think through these issues within the genre of the narrative poem adds additional crinkles to the ball. Why make art about making art about making art? What does it mean to write a representational narrative about an artist's desire to escape representation? And why present this narrative as a prosy free-verse narrative rather than a prose narrative? The poem doesn't resolve these issues; it merely raises them and leaves us with the mic-drop of its final lines:

> The night he was done, the night the ball
> nudged up against the ceiling and his walls
> (a coincidence so long foreseen it has lost its luster)
> he pressed his teeth deep into its surface,
> as a kind of unreadable signature,
> leaned his confused body against it, closed his eyes,
> and, listening to cars pass, wept a little bit.

By highlighting the formal limitations necessary for making art, Yeager suggests that even the most expansive and unruly work must nudge up against its own restrictions, or those of its maker, or those of the environment in which the maker works. Marking the foil ball with an "unreadable signature," the protagonist endorses the piece as pseudo-anonymous representation of himself. Yet what any viewer would see in the reflective surface of the foil is their own image—battered, wrinkled, and warped by the material, like a crumpled-up *Cloud Gate*: that bean-shaped polished-steel sculpture hovering in Chicago's Millenium Park. For Yeager, art engages maker, viewer, and external reality in a messy act of co-creation, pressing together these elements until the artwork signifies only itself.

Too much meditation on aesthetic matters can leave a reader feeling frivolous. As with the anthology contributions from Quintanilla and Borjas discussed above, a strong thematic strain in these pages concerns socio-political issues—another aspect that mirrors contemporary American poetry more broadly. In *Twenty Years of Poem of the Week*, these issues range from military conflict (Hugh Martin's "M16A2 Assault Rifle") to the COVID-19 pandemic (ML Smoker's "Tatogana") and urban poverty (Judy Jordan's sequence "After the Farmer's Market").

Khaled Mattawa's narrative-lyric persona poem "Malouk's Qassida" confronts the African-European migration crisis with linguistic verve and persuasive empathy. This poem plays with the ancient Arabic form of the *qasida* (or *qaṣīdah*)—traditionally a three-part metrical ode that utilizes monorhyme. Over the centuries, the celebratory aspect of the form has altered to accommodate satirical, meditative, and elegiac imitations, including Tennyson's ghazal-like "Locksley Hall."

Mattawa borrows the fictional character of Malouk from the 2014 novel *African Titanics* by Eritrean writer Abu Bakr Khaal. In Mattawa's poem, Malouk, a Nigerian exile, speaks as a representative of his fellow African itinerants on their perilous exodus from Tunisia across the Mediterranean:

MALOUK'S QASSIDA

Lampedusa only a dozen leagues now, the bay
between it and Sousse a corridor of debris,
a Phoenician graveyard.

Are we prepared for the storm's paradise?
The starlings recite the zodiacs on their wings;
the marabouts must in kindness abide.

On the wireless the noises of rescue—
the double dealing of virtue and abuse—
into a theater of salvation we ride.

We are exalted into some hippopotamus,
our mouths checked, hands gloved within
human skin, their fingers inside.

The mouths that speak are covered like the Tuaregs',
their eyes swathed with a dusky mirage.
Our names taken, flicker like fireflies.

Looped around our wrists numbers
that look like a kind of price.
The bullhorns cry, the seagulls deride.

On slippery bridges, we're wrapped in gold foil,
woozy, often diseased. But who is saving whom?
The question's not stated, only implied.

The poem recounts the experience of an ocean extrication most likely by the Italian Navy or an NGO such as the German Sea Watch program. Regardless, Mattawa's "hippopotamus" simile suggests a giant gray maritime vessel that appears menacing yet absurd to the migrants. "Exalted" aboard (from the Latin *exaltare*: "raise, elevate"), Malouk and his comrades experience the cold "salvation" of being prodded, questioned, and barcoded with bracelet "numbers / that look like a kind of price." Malouk experiences further commodification as he's "wrapped in" a thermal blanket's "gold foil" like a "diseased" confection. This inauspicious embarkation results in the culminating question of his journey: "But who is saving whom?"

Malouk's question calls attention to the rapidly shifting cultural and ethnic makeup of the European continent. Europe, which has been experiencing historically low birthrates since the 1960s, has struggled to achieve population stability in all twenty-seven countries. According to Eurostat, only 3.67 million babies were born in the EU in 2023, a 5.4% decrease from 2022. Yet many Europeans favor racist and xenophobic policies that make migration to the continent difficult if not impossible for many people in Malouk's dire position. Such low birth rates and xenophobic policies are shared by other Western countries, including the United States. Migration offers one solution to several geo-political problems. But many Western countries refuse such "salvation" for reasons based not on reason (knowing) but on fear (feeling)— rescuing migrants while turning them away through "the double dealing of virtue and abuse."

Knowing and feeling—the distinction is as essential as the difference between fact and inference. In an aesthetic context, this division recalls M. H. Abrams's *The Mirror and the Lamp*, which offers competing theories of art as a Neoclassical mirror (objectively reflecting reality) and a Romantic lamp (illuminating the subjective self of the maker). Whether Ransom's notion of knowing and feeling influenced Abrams, the idea looms large in a contemporary scene flooded with lax rhythms, haphazard associations, and vague pronouncements typically directed toward an unidentified addressee— that woefully beleaguered lyric "you." If one job of criticism is to define the impediments of appreciating work that a particular age seems to privilege, I confess a desire for more thinking and less emoting from our poets.

One of the many services that this anthology provides is to highlight a few examples of recent American poems that don't blithely conform to the modus operandi of the day. The best poems reprinted in this anthology make plain that contemporary US-American poetry can innovate within traditions of the past while thinking through topics both ancient and current. With any luck, a few of these lines might manage to survive, the way some fragments of Roman verse have lasted for 2,000 years because they were once chiseled as graffiti into a basilica's stone.

—Brian Brodeur
January 7, 2026, Richmond, Indiana

Twenty Years of
Poem of the Week.com

Dilruba Ahmed

GHAZAL

12-8-2020

By no sleight of your hand: I see I've lived on air before.
My heart plummets, a trap-door that was only air before.

Who has not fought love's battles in open air before
never saw your face or took a nom de guerre before.

You arrived in flesh—earthly, a human disguised.
Never so foolishly had I muttered prayers before.

The point's moot if you know my thoughts and I yours
so let skeptics deny we were an unsplit pair before.

Why bridle this love, while wars wear on outside?
Among ruins, my pretense never so threadbare before.

Such love, if your right hand fails, I'll write a score
for your left hand alone, harmonies heard nowhere before.

If the world heard a call, a minaret with no muezzin,
could love overpower what we lived as nightmare before?

Beloved, even pebbles dropped into wells create ripples,
reflecting light where we saw only despair before.

Dilruba Ahmed is the author of *Bring Now the Angels* (Pitt Poetry), with poems featured in *New York Times Magazine*, *The Slowdown*, and *Poetry Unbound*. Her debut book, *Dhaka Dust* (Graywolf), won the Bakeless Prize. Her poems have appeared in *Kenyon Review*, *New England Review*, *Ploughshares*, and *Virginia Quarterly Review*. Her poems have been anthologized in *Best American Poetry*; *Halal If You Hear Me*; *New Moons: Contemporary Writing by North American Muslims*; *They Rise Like A Wave: Asian American Women Poets*; and elsewhere. A long-time educator, Ahmed joined the faculty at Warren Wilson College's MFA Program for Writers in 2021. www.dilrubaahmed.com .

Dan Albergotti

NEITHER

04-22-2015

Her eyes flared like torches. She couldn't understand
how she'd struck me dumb. She couldn't believe,
she said, how I could believe nothing, wouldn't accept
that I would choose annihilation, death over life.

(That's what she said: *death over life*. Said it was a choice.)
She told me her lord stood and knocked and waited
for me to open a door. *It's really a simple choice*, she said.
Everlasting life or eternal death. Which one do you want?

Her eyes flared like torches carried by monks
or by villagers. Her words seemed to float
from her mouth, and her teeth were beautiful.
Isn't that strange, that teeth can be beautiful?

Have you ever looked at a mouth and thought,
Those teeth are beautiful? Have you ever looked at a skull
and thought, *Those teeth are beautiful?* Have you ever thought
about the teeth of a crocodile tearing at the flesh

of an early mammal, crushing bones and flashing white
against primordial mud millennia before the first hominid?
Have you ever thought about all those years of silence?
I didn't want to hurt her as she stood there waiting.

I wanted to say something that would please her,
but I couldn't tell her she was right. She was not right.
She was neither right nor wrong, neither light
nor dark. She was neither angel nor demon, neither dove

nor asp. She was neither the one who could save me
nor the one who could damn me. She was neither
the pearl nor the meal, neither the fossil nor the fir.
She was neither judge nor gem, neither catechism

nor catacomb, neither breath nor body nor fire nor fear
nor yes nor no. She was neither nil nor love
in this half-life world, neither the bomb, nor the flash,
nor the wave that washes everything away.

Well? she said, nearly spitting, her eyes flaring still.
Which . . . one . . . do . . . you . . . want?
And my answer held there, like a flame,
in the deepening silence between us.

Dan Albergotti is the author of *The Boatloads* (BOA Editions, 2008), *Millennial Teeth* (Southern Illinois University Press, 2014), and *Candy* (LSU Press, 2024), as well as the chapbooks *Of Air and Earth* and *Circa MMXX* (Unicorn Press, 2019 and 2022). His poems have appeared widely in such journals as *32 Poems, The Cincinnati Review, Copper Nickel, Ecotone, The Southern Review,* and *The Virginia Quarterly Review.* His work has also been included in *The Best American Poetry, The Pushcart Prize,* and other anthologies.

Rick Barot
TWO VIDEO INSTALLATIONS

03-28-2018

The elephant in the white room
is told to play dead, and she falls

to the gray floor, rocking a little
before going completely still,

only to wake again, rocking again
a few times to find momentum

and push herself onto a splayed
position on the floor, her legs

spread like a skirt, and then
the methodical lifting of each leg

so that each gains its footing,
each lifting her a little until she is

fully up, wholly still once more
until some voice in the room

tells her to die again, all of her
wrinkled bulk made blank canvas,

wet stone for an eye, the camera
moving around her as though

she were the center of a carousel
around which the other animals

galloped and leapt up and brayed.
On another screen, one man's

rapture of grief is told in a face
gone blurry as paint sliding

down a wall, a woman's crying is
an open mouth black with depth,

a woman prays, her hands knotted
into white roots, while another

man standing behind the others
cannot decide whether a howl or

a laugh is what's needed in this
moment after they have been told

to think the worst thing they can
remember, the moment then slowed

to sixteen minutes of quiet film,
so that even the thoughtless blink

of an eye takes a few minutes
to satisfy itself, the pixels changing

like cells under a lens, the last
woman an opera of disbelief about

what has come to pass for them
in the dim room, her face a metal

of rage, the voice somewhere
demanding every form of sorrow

from them, and, having been asked,
this is how they had to answer.

Rick Barot was born in the Philippines and grew up in the San Francisco Bay Area. His fourth book of poems, *The Galleons*, was published by Milkweed Editions and was longlisted for the National Book Award. His earlier collections include *The Darker Fall*, *Want*, which was a finalist for the Lambda Literary Award and won the 2009 Grub Street Book Prize, and *Chord*, all published by Sarabande Books. He has received fellowships from the Guggenheim Foundation, the National Endowment for the Arts, and Stanford University. He lives in Tacoma, Washington and directs The Rainier Writing Workshop, the low-residency MFA program in creative writing at Pacific Lutheran University. His most recent book of poems, *Moving the Bones*, was published by Milkweed Editions in 2024.

Dawn Pichón Barron

MAN CAMPS

03-24-2021

"It's growing faster than any place else in the country," the mayor said with a smile. "It's exciting. It's amazing what oil can do for you. Black Gold."
—Aljazeera.com

"The dark side of the oil boom: Human trafficking in the heartland"
—Aaron Ernst

Williston, I beg you to be a woman
To understand the breaking of hearts
And children. You are not; and I grieve
Oiled human tears for
How could you not know what would happen
With all those men? Men have not civilized
Themselves when they have drugs, alcohol,
Money to burn, anger to churn and seek
Release. Release, you know:
Hitting something, hurting something, fucking something
Turns out that something is a Sum One. A girl, a boy,
A woman. Yours, his, mine ours.
Bakken, a shale rock formation, now run through
By greed and gluttony. To be used, discarded, and
Folded into a burned memory. And when the Black Gold
Is gone, the shame will follow you; the broken will be left
Behind to fossilize their grief.

Dawn Pichón Barron (she/her) is a mixt-blood Indigi-Euro writer & scholar born in Southern California and primarily raised in rural Spokane. She is the academic director of the Native Pathways Program and member of the Faculty at The Evergreen State College. Dawn is thrilled to participate in state-wide artist promotion and sustainment as an Artist Trust Board Member. Her work can be found in *Yellow Medicine Review*, *Pittsburgh Poetry Review*, *Moss*, *Pontoon*, the anthology *Of A Monstrous Child* (Lost Horse Press, 2011), her chapbook *ESCAPE GIRL BLUES* (Finishing Line Press, 2018), in the anthology *A Socially Just Classroom: Transdisciplinary Approaches to Teaching Writing Across the Humanities* (Vernon Press, 2022) and elsewhere. She lives with her saltwater mermxn & chihuahuas in the sometimes sunny Pacific NW, at the southern tip of the Salish Sea on the stolen ancestral homelands of the tribal bands and clans of the Medicine Creek Treaty (1854).

Zeina Hashem Beck

MESSAGE FROM MY AUNT ON HER SON'S DEATH ANNIVERSARY

08-27-2018

My aunt, the one who has lost a son
to a shooting on the street, the one slowly losing
her sight, sends me voice messages and emoticons,
prayers like *A fortress, my love,*
protect you from harm in all directions-
above and below you, behind and before you.

Today, the emoticon is an orange.
Perhaps it's a mistake. Perhaps she means
a kiss, or a heart, or a flower,
her eyes and aging fingers failing her.

But perhaps she means the fruit, remembers
how she used to sing me that song
where I was the orange she wanted
to peel and eat and not share with anyone,

remembers how much I love sour winter oranges,
the way they are round and whole, yet break
into the many bright crescents hidden beneath their skin.

Perhaps she's saying what she always says
when she opens her arms and walks toward me,
I was telling myself you must have arrived.
The whole town smells of oranges when you are here.

Zeina Hashem Beck is a Lebanese poet. Her collection of 40 palindromic sonnets, titled *This Was Supposed to Be About Beauty*, is forthcoming from Penguin Poets in Spring 2027. She's the winner of the 2023 Arab American Book Award for Poetry for *O*, which was named a Best Book of the Year by Literary Hub and The New York Public Library. She's also the author of *Louder than Hearts* and *To Live in Autumn*, as well as the chapbooks *3arabi Song* and *There Was and How Much There Was*. Her work has appeared in *LARB*, *Lithub*, *The Nation*, *Academy of American Poets*, and elsewhere. She's the co-editor, with Hala Alyan, of the anthology *We Call to the Eye and the Night: Love Poems by Writers of Arab Descent*. She's the co-creator and co-host, with poet Farah Chamma, of Maqsouda, a podcast in Arabic about Arabic poetry. Zeina currently resides in California.

Sheila Black

RADIUM DREAM

08-25-2025

We come at the wrong time of year by a hair
or a week, and the brown birds flying onward,
out of reach. My son tilts his head. A minor star-
burst of cranes lights the far corner of
the sky—stragglers, fewer than expected,
but enough to glitter the air with strangeness—
these birds with their necks not tucked in, forming
their odd cries. When they land by the shore,
their toothpick legs appear hardly enough
to hold up their robust bodies. Often

I think—"That's not really happening is it?" as though I
were acting in a film or a vision of a life. On the
highway, they warn us not to drink—too much
uranium, leached down from the abandoned mines.
The cranes twist their necks to stab the quick-
light of fish. Do cranes know how to
swim? And why is swimming so different than flying?

Now, aloft again, they apparate with uncanny
quickness into cloud. How does the eye lose
them—is it how high they rise? The bones

in my son's hand, they tell me, have stopped growing
too early. They act like this is a problem, but I
have radium dreams—a brightness: Him, me, you, the
cranes, and in them nothing dies.

Sheila Black is the author of five poetry collections and three chapbooks, most recently *For the Loneliness of Walking Out* (Lily Poetry Review Books, 2025). Poems and essays have appeared in *Blackbird*, *Kenyon Review Online*, *Poetry*, *The Nation*, and *The New York Times*. She is assistant director of the Virginia G. Piper Center for Creative Writing at ASU.

Kimberly M. Blaeser

THIS STRANGER'S BEAUTY

04-21-2021

Barely formed fetus feet and tiny Spock ears
Ripley's surreal—this listing on the edge of small perfection;
pink mouse pup bald and suckling blindly from the doe
feeding as we all do on the driven milk of becoming.

Somewhere beneath the sealed lumps of black eyes
a swimming to awareness under the stretched membrane of skin,
you a mere half gram and every pore and wrinkle a vanity
of knowing your own ghostly poetry, your fragility.

Everywhere we look—whimsy and a holy clamor for survival:
wolf spiderlings cling like moss to their mother's back
while guppies and even angelfish gulp their fry
and still my lonely violin heart tunes to frog song,

to wolf howl and loon calls and other darker matter.
I believe in the fluid arch of frill-necked lizards,
impossible serrated swirls, like cirque de soleil
Seeker's eels. All a reptilian anti-splendor—*the horror.*

The heart of darkness illuminated by small gods
or blind and relentless human hunger for beauty,
as if each striped haunch and stretch were our own
each turquoise spot the simple reversal of revulsion.

We know contortion of birth, our own grotesque
sad embrace of air, of gravity. The slither and purple weight
of voice, the awakening flex of body. Hold this strange light—
a relentless spilling of fever over the untrammeled earth.

Kimberly Blaeser, past Wisconsin Poet Laureate and founding director of Indigenous Nations Poets, is the author of six poetry collections—including *Ancient Light.* An Anishinaabe activist and environmentalist from White Earth Nation, Blaeser is a Prof. Emerita at University of Wisconsin–Milwaukee and an MFA faculty member at Institute of American Indian Arts.

Tommye Blount

AMERICANA ELEGY

11-9-2020

Less boy, more band,
more twang, less bling,

less hip-hop, on brand,
more opry, less bang,
less cornrows, more corn-

field, spiritual, less house,
more plantation, a shorn

image, more downhome,
more green, more blue
sky, more bluegrass,

less rhythm, less
blues, more church pew,

more cross, less hood,
more hood, more white
washed denim, less back-

lash, more goldenrod,
less ballad, more lyric,

less gold grills, less rap
sheet, more sheet music,
less trap beat, less trap

beat, more poplar,
less popular, a more authentic timbre,

more big game, more field
dressing, more lake,
more master—control.

Tommye Blount was born and raised in Detroit. He holds an MFA from Warren Wilson College, and is the author of *Fantasia for the Man in Blue* (Four Way Books, 2020), a finalist for the National Book Award, and the chapbook *What Are We Not For* (Bull City Press, 2016). Blount is the recipient of scholarships and fellowships from Kresge Arts in Detroit and the Bread Loaf Writers' Conference. In 2023, he received a Whiting Award in Poetry. A Cave Canem Fellow, Blount lives in Novi, Michigan.

Kristin Bock

THE DREAMING RIFLE

09-01-2025

RIBBON

I am speaking to you from the end
of the flat world by a waterfall

that plummets all the way to Pluto,
where silence and dream pass like ships

and are gone. This is how you live
when you have nothing left

to hold onto. Up all night, I listen
to something drag its trap closer.

I tie myself into knots at the thought
of the girl who left as softly as a silhouette

at dawn. Out the open window, I watch
a doe step into the wide field, her breath,

cool and blue, blooms like morning
glories on the trellis—all those pendulous,

poisonous seeds within reach.
Despite the silk and slight of me,

she can see me
swinging from the sill by daybreak.

DRESS AND RIBBON

I feel empty, says the dress to the ribbon. *I know*, says the ribbon to the dress, stretching her blueness across the vanity. It's cold, the window wide open in December. Outside, the moon is big and yellow, clouds slipping apart like petticoat seams. *Where is the girl and her delicate hands?* says the dress. *I don't know*, says the ribbon. *Remember her voice, the song she sang about a swing and a boy?* A sheet tied to the bedpost billows like a sail. *I remember her singing sadly to the moon*, says the dress. *Yes*, says the ribbon. *Her hair was as silky as moth wings. I could barely hang on.*

DAWN

Rising from a garden bed,
       I stumble over bodies

still asleep in the grass,
       spear my blue silk blouse

on the spires of pines, bleed
       across the vaulted clouds,

and vanish into the orchard
       where my tiny feet

leave a crooked trail

       of black seeds

down the slip-

       pery

          spiral

staircase

       of an apple.

DOVECOTE

Gunshots from the woods
cause a fierce fluttering—

Brooklyn, Stella, Emma

Like warm water, they blow
right through me.

Ella, Anna, Shelly

The lost become doves
before they are found

Dottie, Jody, Jada

in a ditch, in the deep
folds of a meadow.

Mary, Amber, Sherry

A limbo
of afternoons for

Hayley, Hannah, Pearl

If you cup your hand
and blow into it, you will know

Ava, Isabelle, Mia

the burden of a soul. I am
a house built of sad lines,

Luna, Grace, Lily

my side broken open
to the moon. Inside me,

Alice, Allie, Ivy

a stem, some seeds,
a button, a ribbon blue—

the weight of things
sown and flown.

RAIN

In a summer growing cold
Queen Anne's lace

are snowflakes. Hard grapes,
thirsty bees—a beast

in the waterdark leaves. Light
grows black with knowing

long shadows at the end of day.
There is an immense meadow

inside us. O to close
like the spent cups of flowers!

We the fallen, we the risen,
we the lidless, we the rain.

DOVECOTE AND RAIN

Dovecote: Give me wind, lightning's crude language across the sky.

Rain: We fall like bolts of silk onto the faces of poppies. Like threaded stars into the thirsty mouth of the cistern.

Dovecote: You are a lover stroking me with a million small mirrors. Who else are you?

Rain: We are talons on the tin roof of a barn, vapors of spirits in the still.

Dovecote: What do you see tonight?

Rain: Everything. I see a farmer stumbling from his still, ripping his fist across the teeth of his boy.

Dovecote: The grass feels like razors when the wind picks up.

Rain: I see the boy sneaking moonshine for the pain, lurching through flooded fields to throw stones at a farmhouse window. I see a girl sliding a blue ribbon from her gold-red hair, night dress falling to her waist.

Dovecote: Does the boy see her?

Rain: She's a warbled ghost behind wet glass.

Dovecote: Can you see the dead fluttering inside me?

Rain: We hear them. Cries issue from their fluted bones. Like windchimes, they wish to be ravished.

Dovecote: How they long for the distillation of the soul! Can you save them?

Rain: No. Never.

Dovecote: Can you tell the future?

Rain: Yes, we live in cycles.

Dovecote: What becomes of the boy?

Rain: We see his face reflected in the cistern, six bird bones for a mouth.

Dovecote: And of the girl?

Rain: We see a dove weaving its nest with strands of her hair left golden in the ropes of a swing.

Dovecote: How will I know her?

Rain: Listen for the sound of hammering between two mountains, then a cry like no other.

RIFLE

I wake inside the hollow
of an oak, the sun leaking

behind the field trees. Slowly at first,
the body is hauled skyward,

lifting her from the mouth of
a weeping cistern, her hair

heavy, dripping like ropes
undone. Her spring feet

dangling like a ragdoll towed

by a toddler, wearily to sleep.

From the swarm of flashing
lights, someone emerges to turn

her blowfly body face-up. It's occupied.
Tenanted. Accompanied.

No longer alone. Had I a twilight
in which she could have hidden.

Had I a cloven dovecote or a field
of forgotten bathtubs—

crazed, clawfooted, filling
with rainwater and just her size.

A short poem cuts right to the heart. I like its precision, its directness, its audacity if you will. The short poem has to pack a powerful punch or it will be lost. I remember reading "The Death of the Ball Turret Gunner" by Jarrell as a teenager and being floored by it. I couldn't believe how deeply I could be moved by language in just 5 short lines. From then on, I've always been drawn to short, highly imagistic poems that seem to be successful at marrying idea and image. I always thought the Imagist movement faded too soon. Pound said "use no superfluous word, no adjective, which does not reveal something" and that's a philosophy that may not be completely realistic, but one I've aspired to my whole writing life. This poem is a stitched together sequence of short poems. The power of each short burst is intended to carry throughout the entire piece.

Kristin Bock is the author of two collections of poetry published by Tupelo Press: *Cloisters* (2008) and *Glass Bikini* (2020). Her work was featured in *The Best American Poetry 2022* and is forthcoming in *The Surreal-Absurd Anthology*, due for publication by Mercurius Press in July 2025. A Massachusetts Cultural Council fellow, she holds an MFA in poetry from the University of Massachusetts, Amherst where she teaches Business Communication. She lives in Western, MA with her husband and together they restore liturgical art. This is an excerpt from a collaborative chapbook in progress, written with poet and artist, L.I. Henley: *The Dreaming Rifle*, an anti-pastoral and lyrical fable centered around the disappearance of a young, teenage girl told by a chorus of animated objects—a scythe, a clawfoot bathtub, a rifle, a field of red poppies, etc. The choir of voices acts as unreliable witnesses, as jury, and as sorrowful chroniclers of an all-too-common occurrence. Slowly, the voices reveal the girl's story while also posing questions about the reader's complicity in systemic violence. Visit Kristin at https://kristinbock.mystrikingly.com and follow her on Instagram @kbock777.

Dexter L. Booth

CONVERSATION STARTERS OR THINGS I'D NEVER SAY TO YOU IN PUBLIC

11-24-2015

—for R.A.

False: Napoleon didn't shoot off the nose of the Great Sphinx of Giza.
The truth is humbling: the Sufi Sheik, Sayim al- Dahr blew up the nose
because, of course, any statue of a negro's face that large
must have been idolatrous.

These are my thoughts on Halloween night,
two-thirds into a bottle of Syrah, 20,000 miles
from home, and dressed in zombie latex that
only came in two shades of Caucasian. All this glue
and the wounds won't stick. All this fake
blood and brown Sharpie so I can tell
everyone I am a dead black guy
resurrected by the White Man Virus,
and you'll laugh.

At the end of the night Christine's friend will
take photos on the porch, after a moment
of focusing his camera say, "I can't see you,"
to which I'll responded.

That, sir, is racist.

It is a joke. It is a Sufi Sheik-Napoleon cannon-bomb
that has nothing to do with height, the number
of men you've seduced, the fact
that our lives are just expansion
and cooling; we are

the after effect of the Big Bang.

17

But I digress,
it is dark, and I am drunk.
I am drunk and you, dressed
as a bride's maid, wearing six inch heels.
It is dark and we are friends
and I am inebriated enough for it to be
awkward that your breasts are
where I am used to seeing your eyes.
You, suddenly my height, and still
pleasant. So unlike Stripper Nick,
who will later say
he is going to college in CA to major
in brewing beer. Less than a year ago
he was one of two men fighting for your
bed in a bar parking lot.

And there's Fernando
who two years past
dressed as a banana
but tonight is a panda
or a Hispanic guy in black face,
all excessively sexual
depending on your B.A.C.
and sense of humor.

This of course returns
to the dark. Scientists say that
if the universe keeps growing
outward the notion of a star
will be millennial mythology.

Imagine looking up and thinking
 the Earth is the only thing...

Dexter L. Booth is the author of *Abracadabra, Sunshine* (Red Hen Press, 2021) and *Scratching the Ghost* (Graywolf Press, 2013). His poems have been included in numerous anthologies including *The Burden of Light: Poems on Illness and Loss*, *The Golden Shovel Anthology* honoring Gwendolyn Brooks, *Furious Flower: Seeding the Future of African American Poetry*, and *The Future of Black: Afrofuturism, Black Comics, and Superhero Poetry*. Booth holds an MFA from Arizona State University and a Ph.D. from the University of Southern California.

Sara Borjas

POCHA CAFÉ

02-14-2023

Here, we use Cholula, not homemade salsa.
We'll serve corn tortillas with your bacon and eggs.
You can ask what is in *everything* instead of just
eating it. We know you Pochas love to do that.

Enjoy a quesadilla with American cheese!
Or nachos we prepare in our brother's hand-me-down
microwave he gave us when he joined the Air Force
or just a flour tortilla spread with butter. Here, we listen

to War, Smokey, Selena, The Smiths and Art Laboe!
Let's dedicate everything to our incarcerated cousins
serving bullshit sentences in Wasco and Corcoran
and Chowchilla State Prisons but we never put money

on their books or write them. At Pocha Café, we play
Blood in Blood Out and *Stand and Deliver* and mistake
someone's dad on the daily for Edward James Olmos.
Even we think all Mexicans looks alike, or that all Latinos

are Mexican and that's why our Salvadorian
and Boricua homies talk shit but that's what people do
when they love you so fuck it! If you are a downright
cultural traitor, come on in! Here, at Pocha Café

we only order rice and don't speak Spanish so we
don't get corrected and we *stay out the fuckin kitchen*
like our mamas told us and we refuse lemons
and corridos in solidarity. Except when we are

completely wasted drunk—then we can listen to "El Rey"
and drink Victoria and embrace our stretched souls'
befuddled half-ass gritos. If you don't know the words
to "El Rey" because you don't speak Spanish,

19

just make up non sense words and sing the hook
because you've been drinking and you love that shit.
You speak better Spanish when drunk, anyways. Or,
you only speak it drunk because sober you

doesn't want that colonizer's language anyways!
You ain't about colonizing the self, you're about
decolonizing your consciousness, your morality,
your diet, your love. Speaking of pain, come listen

to "Amor Eterno" and step on each other's
dirty Converse. Let's be resentful about how
we didn't have a quinceanera and forget
that we never wanted one until we were sophomores

in state colleges when we took a Chicano Studies class
and gave ourselves a Nahuatl name and joined Mecha.
Let's never mention how we thought the big dresses
and gold chains and placas were tacky, or how

we were too ashamed to wear anything that made us
look proud of ourselves. Oh what? You're having a baby
shower and your son is turning two? Come celebrate
at Pocha Café with our never-ending beer package!

You have a padrino for the beer right? We might be
understaffed but your children know how to garnish
your beers, we're sure. In fact, they might be drinking
already because some primo you call Johnny

or Mike or Bill but whose real names are Juan
and Miguel and Guillermo is telling them
to be a man or trying to get them drunk so they
can kiss them behind your tio's work truck

in the driveway while everyone is in the backyard
listening to 2 Live Crew. Come to Pocha Café
and expropriate your Pochaism as an act
of empowerment! Let's complement each other

on how articulate we are like white teachers at school.
Fuck it, let's listen to country music and sing-cry!
Let's mess up the cholo handshake because even
our muscle memory forgot our bodies and this way

our folks can feel better about themselves
when they judge us! Orale! Simon! Let's find affinity
in canned menudo, in cilantro with the stems
all in it, in the pig's foot that grosses out half of us

and makes the other half of us feel Mexican for once.
Gather up all your impurities, your Anglicized names,
all your anxiety attacks and bad accents,
your scraps of culture and half-bred shame

and put on your dickies and your gold loop
earrings and come lend us your broken Spanish!
Come get drunk enough to tell your dad you love him
and your brother-in-law to finally fuck off! Come be

the part of yourself that scares the entire family!
All you Pochas! You might know who you are.

SARA BORJAS is a Xicanx pocha from Turtle Island before it was stolen and its people were genocided and colonized. She is a Fresno poet. Her debut collection of poetry, *Heart Like a Window, Mouth Like a Cliff* was published by Noemi Press in 2019 and won a 2020 American Book Award. Sara was named one of *Poets & Writers* 2019 Debut Poets and has received fellowships from MacDowell, CantoMundo, The Poetry Foundation and others. Her work can be found in *AGNI: To Never Have Risked Our Lives: A Portfolio of Central American and Mexican Diaspora Writing*, *The Rumpus*, *The Gettysburg Review*, *Catapult*, *Ploughshares*, *Poem-a-Day* by The Academy of American Poets, *Alta* and *The Offing*, amongst others. She teaches innovative undergraduates at CSU East Bay, believes that all Black lives matter and all Palestinian lives matter and will resist white supremacy and settler colonialism until Black liberation is realized and Palestine is free. Sara lives in Oakland and stays rooted in Fresno. find her @ saraborhaz or at www.saraborjas.com. Say their names.

Mark J. Brewin

BURNING DOWN THE CAMPER

02-05-2014

For seven days my father scavenged the junked camper.
He deveined copper wiring from walls, took sledge hammer,
crowbar and cat's paw to kitchenette cabinets.
His shunted boot buckled doorjambs. His hands
split sewage lines and salvaged the propane stove top.

For seven days, while dismantling the rank trailer—
wrist deep in the musk of petrified mouse carcasses
and sun-cooked frog bodies, insect shells littered along sills—
he longed for the bonfire's shape: farm crates and splintered rafters,
taproots and runners for kindling. The way it would all blaze.

He tore brass knobs from drawers, screws from lumber.
And after seven days, on his weekend off
from the electric utility, he warehoused the wanted parts
in the garage loft and exchanged his scrap iron cash
for two cases of Milwaukee's Best. He piled the RV shards

in a heap—layering house trash, wire casings,
Styrofoam cooler chunks—and hollered for the family to watch
the flames from bare cable spools in the backyard. My mother,
cradling my infant brother, said no, but my sister and I
scrambled beyond the back porch and bobbled around the pit,

waved sunflower stalks like wands over the tattered flames,
chanted gibberish incantations, and with each Abracadabra!
our father would chuck empties into the glowing center.
Raking the coals with a bean stake, he stammered facts:
that the worst hell glow is not orange, but white;

that liquefied dinosaurs filled our minivan's gas tank;
that—if we wanted—we could spit on the blistering steel
and watch the dribble vanish, so long as we didn't get too close.
So, we mustered saliva, hocked as much as children could, laughed.
But our father with other plans for pleasing his audience,

stumbled from the shed, kicking sandbox toys and Wiffle Ball bats
to where we sat and promised us we would see magic.
He moved a plastic alligator closer to the heat, until
an inch away, its jaws melted, eyebrows and paws puddled
on the bare earth, and we wanted more. Wads of Sunday circulars

flared green, burning gas station coffee cups gave off a pitch smoke.
Window screens shriveled and glass panes burst.
Two-liter cola bottles, after a flash from the garden hose,
collapsed in on themselves as if ghost wrung. He used
words like vacuum and pressure. They meant nothing.

By bedtime, all that remained were more beer cans and rubble
coughing up ash, embers giving way to the match heads of stars.
A night dirge. The pucker and fizz of singed wreck.
My mother called for my sister and me to come in,
but my father—enjoying his dawdling children—yelled back

that we were just fine so long as he could stand.
Words turned to marbles in his mouth. The way he spoke
our names, a muttered hex. His guttural song
kept us awake, cursing the power plant and its graveyard shift,
as he entertained his kids with a homemade sacrifice of shrubs,

mowed grass, crumbling shed roof and front deck cross beams.
The knot and grain of stubble around his chin.
The stock and rings of work callusing his hands and fingers.
A shit camper. Hulk and debris rescued from house repairs
and fix-it jobs, good for one last thing: The mystical.
The power in anything that will burn.

Mark Jay Brewin Jr's first book *Scrap Iron* won the 2012 Agha Shahid Ali Poetry Prize
at the University of Utah Press. His poems have been featured in *Antioch Review, Beloit
Poetry Journal, The Cortland Review, Fugue, The Missouri Review Online, North American
Review, Prairie Schooner, Sycamore Review, Southern Humanities Review, Tahoma
Literary Review,* and elsewhere. In Spring of 2026, he will be teaching poetry with
Little Nice Workshops in Lincoln, Rhode Island. He happily resides in Easthampton,
Massachusetts with his wife, Jess, and son, Barnaby.

Bill Brown

ELEMENTAL

01-19-2016

What the river says, that is what I say
—William Stafford

I.

On the Tellico River, rocks that shape
the water's flow grow smooth and undercut
by this myriad force. At night, shadowed
by sycamore and birch, wherever current
brushes stone, shivers a glow. Light from
distant stars and our squat moon shimmers
Bald River Falls, perhaps tricks natural
selection and our mammalian optic nerve
to accept this magic as just an evening
beside a mountain stream the Cherokee
claim as holy.

II.

Memory changes the narrative:
Your grandmother teaching you
how to tight-line fish without a cork.
It's in the feel of the pole, the line tension—
what's in the water on the other end—
the slight lift of wrist when the jerk comes—
all with early willow green—how it can't
be separated in the moment-the elements—
stone outcrop, light in trees, the river—
how an old woman made of flesh commands
such resolve—flesh, mostly water, mineral—
light and shadow, brushstrokes in the eyes,
nuance of voice. My father loved Rivers
as much as Jesus—the Buffalo, the Duck,
the Caney Fork, the Tennessee, time there,

earthly sacraments of something he knew eternal.
Why so much hoodoo about heaven
when the river and this life demand our praise.

III.

River, how rain pocks your moving surface—
little rings swirling just enough to confuse
the clouds, as tall reeds at your bank form
green sleeves. And how polished rocks
beneath the shallow shoals sing for you.
My wife cracked the windows and your
breeze-song entered sleep like camphor,
as if night held seashells to our ears. You
are blind to what my eyes gather from your
surface, and yet I use the second person
as if you understood my syllabic babble.
But you speak a language old as stone.
I sit on your bank and glimpse the everlasting,
as a moon rises red through dark limbs,
turns yellow, and brightens every eddy
and current swirl—a moon you can draw
water from, its lunar drift in every pail.

Bill Brown is the author of ten collections of poetry and a writing textbook on which he collaborated with Malcolm Glass. During the past thirty years, he has published hundreds of poems and articles in college journals, magazines, and anthologies. In 1999, Brown wrote and co-produced the Instructional Television Series, *Student Centered Learning*, for Nashville Public Television. Since 1983, Brown directed the writing program at Hume-Fogg Academic High School in Nashville. He retired from Hume-Fogg in May, 2003 and accepted a part-time lecturer's position at Peabody College of Vanderbilt University. In 1995, the National Foundation for Advancement in the Arts named him Distinguished Teacher in the Arts. He has been a Scholar in Poetry at the Bread Loaf Writers Conference, a Fellow at the Virginia Center for the Creative Arts, and a two-time recipient of Fellowships in poetry from the Tennessee Arts Commission. In 2011, the Tennessee Writers Alliance awarded Brown: Writer of the Year.

Derrick Weston Brown

THE ROOT, A HAIBUN FOR D'ANGELO

03-18-2019

D, when you dropped Brown Sugar, I already knew you were a legend, before I sliced away the plastic wrap from your CD with my index finger's nail. Before I dropped your disc, that should have been vinyl, into my player, that should have been a hi-fi, I opened the booklet and read the liner notes. You were Richmond, by way of Chesapeake, by way of James River, by way of current, axis, axe handle, and Pentecostal "Rock me Jesus" heave. You were a choir child, a PK, till you traded Emmanuel for Camille, Jehovah for Jaime Starr. A Prince for a Prince.

Beneath the hymnal
Rapture makes the organ groan
Lord we must confess

D,
I turned three discmen into smoking husks playing your album.
-Had heard whispers of your coming within the liner notes of Tribe's Midnight Marauders. Heard you wrote "U Will Know" for the Jason's Lyric soundtrack, and then I chanced upon an early duet between you and Badu, your voices cane sugar raw and wet. She, the Tammi to your Marvin, "Your Precious Love" a throw-away on another obscure movie soundtrack. But Brown Sugar begat "Lady" begat "Smooth" begat "When We Get By", "Shit, Damn, Muthafucka". I raised a woman's hem in a dorm room hallway to track one, and by the first cycle (had your album on repeat) my virginity was a satin pillow slip cover, eased off and discarded, never missed.

Sophomore meets Junior
Our tarheel tongues hurricane
Yourrrr Myyy Laaadeee

Chico DeBarge was that bullshit. And soon enough, everybody was eating off your plate. But then you disappeared for a while. We had Maxwell though, which is like comparing pecans to brazil nuts. Cat had the finesse, the croon, but you had that Mason jar shit. Maxwell was a sweaty

Brooklyn stoop, but you were muggy southern late August sharecropping heat, slow dragging up front porches

and pushing through screen doors. Word was you weren't dropping an album for a while and then   Voodoo.   Nigga.

Prince went and got saved, but you Archangel, Melchizidek, Michael, here you come with your blown bulb afro, guitar, and a body chiseled with abs that had to be cut from black obelisks!? Nigga! Elekes!? Cuba? Talkin bout roots and thangs!? D!? Where you been?

Nineteen Ninety Nine
One breath from Apocalypse
Pass the Chicken Grease

Your album cut deep D. There was a bruise in your music. Somehow love had turned to incense ash in your hands. I heard the beginning of the Soulquarians in the folds of your groove. Questlove was in the studio, Meth, Red, Roy Hargrove, Clapton, and some wunderkind from Detroit named Dilla.

Your album never left my car or my CD case D. The Root, Devil's Pie, Send It On, Untitled/How Does It Feel? I tried to write a poetic equivalent, tried to finger paint your funk on pages. No sir. No Luck. But one late night, beyond the wasp nest thin walls of my first apartment, I heard a couple push and press out a multi-syllabic rendition of your whole album. Know that people made the type of Love, the type of Fuck to your music, that in 50 years will still make them look at their partner and say, "Who the hell were you that night?" Ah. D. You had that pinnacle shit sewn. I wanted an encore but then you vanished again.

I heard you got fat. Heard hated the cat calls and shrieks for your flesh, and only flesh. It was the video that did you in, not to mention the coke, the liquor, and that hulking menace you felt stalking you in that dark maw just beyond the stage lights. That monster, gnawed Marvin, Cooke, and Donny into bits of blood and biography. Then, there were years of rumors, arrests and mug shots, and the day your SUV swerved, buckled and spit you out across the asphalt highway like suspect dice.

D,

We lost Lauryn (we never had her). Barry's gone, Issac, Dennis, Gerald, Luther, Michael, Michael, Michael, then Whitney, we lost Aretha. Did you ever meet Amy? And then you return, a jig sawed Osiris, pieced together by guitar string, scar tissue and song.

What you call a man
who courts death and plays music
D'Angelo

Derrick Weston Brown holds an MFA in Creative Writing from American University. He is the founding Poet-In-Residence of Busboys and Poets. He is a graduate of the Cave Canem and VONA summer workshops. He has received fellowships and scholarships to attend residencies such as The Community of Writers and The Virginia Center for the Creative Arts. He has been the recipient of an individual artist grant from the Maryland State Arts Council and was awarded the E. Lynn Harris Impact Award from the Hurston/Wright Foundation in 2023. His work has been published and featured in such print journals and online publications as *Racebaitr, Colorlines,* and *The Magazine of Fantasy & Science Fiction.* His work has been widely anthologized in such esteemed collections as *The Future of Black: Afrofuturism, Black Comics and Superhero Poetry, A Face to Meet the Faces: An Anthology of Contemporary Persona Poetry, Dear Yusef: Essays, Letters and Poems for and About One Mr. Yusef Komunyakaa, Furious Flower: Seeding the Future of African-American Poetry.* His debut collection of poetry, *Wisdom Teeth* was released in 2011 through PM Press. His second collection of poetry, a chapbook entitled *On All Fronts,* was released along with two other poetry chapbooks in a bound series from Upper Rubber Boot Press entitled *Floodgates Vol.5,* March of 2019. He is full-time Creative Writing faculty of the Cinematic Arts and Media Production (C.A.M.P.) department at The Duke Ellington School of the Arts.

Nickole Brown

A PRAYER TO TALK TO ANIMALS

09-20-2022

Lord, I ain't asking to be the Beastmaster
gym-ripped in a jungle loincloth
or a Doctor Dolittle or even the expensive vet
down the street, that stethoscoped redhead,
her diamond ring big as a Cracker Jack toy.
All I want is for you to help me flip
off this lightbox and its scroll of dread, to rip
a tiny tear between this world and that, a slit
in the veil, Lord, one of those old-fashioned peeping
keyholes through which I can press my dumb
lips and speak. If you will, Lord, make me the teeth
hot in the mouth of a raccoon scraping
the junk I scraped from last night's plates,
make me the blue eye of that young crow cocked to
me—too selfish to even look up from the flash
of my damn phone. Oh, forgive me, Lord,
how human I've become, busy clicking
what I like, busy pushing
my cuticles back and back to expose
all ten pale, useless moons. Would you let me
tell your creatures how sorry
I am, let them know exactly
what we've done? Am I not an animal
too? If so, Lord, make me one again.
Give me back my dirty claws and blood-warm
horns, braid back those long-
frayed strands of every nerve tingling
with all I thought I had to do today.
Fork my tongue, Lord. There is a sorrow on the air
I taste but cannot name. I want to open
my mouth and know the exact
flavor of what's to come, I want to open
my mouth and sound a language
that calls all language home.

Nickole Brown received her MFA from the Vermont College of Fine Arts, studied literature at Oxford University, and was the editorial assistant for the late Hunter S. Thompson. She worked at Sarabande Books for ten years. She's the author of *Sister*, first published in 2007 with a new edition reissued in 2018. Her second book, *Fanny Says* (BOA Editions), won the Weatherford Award for Appalachian Poetry in 2015. Currently, she lives in Asheville, NC, where she volunteers at several different animal sanctuaries. Since 2016, she's been writing about these animals, resisting the kind of pastorals that made her (and many of the working-class folks from the Kentucky that raised her) feel shut out of nature and the writing about it. *To Those Who Were Our First Gods*, a chapbook of these first nine poems, won the 2018 Rattle Prize, and her essay-in-poems, *The Donkey Elegies*, was published by Sibling Rivalry Press in 2020. Her poem "Parable" won the 2024 Treehouse Climate Action Poem Prize and was published as part of the Academy of American Poet's Poem-a-Day initiative. Every summer, she teaches as part of the low-residency MFA Program at the Sewanee School of Letters in Tennessee. She's a proud fellow of the Black Earth Institute and is President of the Hellbender Gathering of Poets, a nonprofit organization that aims to nurture a community hellbent on finding the words that protect and repair our climate-changed world.

J. Scott Brownlee

INTO THE VALLEY OAK THAT WILL NOT SING, THAT WILL NOT EVEN TALK

08-25-2016

We commend the spirits
of dead cows whose bones
bleach in the cruel radiance
of the sun god Ra's land,
these Egyptian pastures.
Mirages melt salt pyramids
at the edge of escarpment
and cedar thicket. Snag
yourself on a limb or a great-
horned owl's call navigating
back roads or the guitar music
at the local pool shack
referred to as "a bar"
despite only Shiner
in its beverage coolers.
The drunk dart players spin
on their axes of booze,
smoke, and country lyrics
but remain beautiful
in their constant twirling
back into each other.
Have you ever watched them?
Have you ever listened
to the sermon of bodies
relaxed and laughing?
To commune as they do
you must give up
your good life, the city,
the Q train, Park Slope,
and pizza. Traveler,
settle here if you know
what work is and cannot
escape it without feeling guilty.
Come and teach school
at least. You're the man

with two wives caught
between deciding—
the two cities you keep
like two young families
who don't know each other
though they met on the 4th
of July at the fireworks
show in this two-bit
county that includes Llano,
Kingsland, and part of a vast
lake that touches the sky
when you stand beside it
as the thunderheads build
the same blue erasure
they are building today
with their ruthless anvils.
Disappear here and no one
will ever find you. Steal
a truck and head out on 16
to the coast, or the border,
or hell—drive wherever
you want with the lover
you miss and have not
written yet but will write
to today when the rainfall
ceases, and you're left
in a Ford with some paper,
a pen, and your fingertips
inked blue as if dipped
in blood from a vein
in your arm extending
for miles if you stretch it out
in your imagination all the way
from Brooklyn to your heart
in Texas: just the way you like it.

J. Scott Brownlee is a poet from Llano, Texas and former Writers in the Public Schools fellow at NYU, where he taught creative writing and completed an MFA. He is the author of the chapbooks *Highway or Belief, Ascension,* and *On the Occasion of the Last Old Camp Meeting in Llano County.* Honors for these collections include the 2013 Button Poetry Prize, 2014 Robert Phillips Poetry Prize, and 2015 Tree Light Books Prize. His first full-length collection, *Requiem for Used Ignition Cap,* was a finalist for the National Poetry Series and 2015 Writers' League of Texas Book Award and selected by C. Dale Young as the winner of the 2015 Orison Poetry Prize. It also won the 2016 Best first Book of Poetry Award from the Texas Institute of Letters. His second full-length collection, *What Flesh Inherits,* will be published in fall 2026 by Texas Review Press. He currently splits time between Austin, Asheville, Brooklyn, and Llano, and teaches for Brooklyn Poets as a core faculty member.

Lauren Camp

TO FAIL AND FAIL AND STILL GO ON

09-05-2023

Sunrise. Tight roads
hew to a line
of Sitka. Gatekeepers, gray scaffold.

Agnes Martin burned her paintings.
For twenty years, she painted and for twenty years
she made them
ash. Someone in the kitchen called this ambition.

Tonight, we build a fire.
Sit on wooden chairs, a wire bench.

Where a mouth might enter
one solitude follows another, ready to loosen.

A man smokes a cigar: fingers the fume.
In the pit, flames bend
and funnel. I say very little, watch the red

sparks spit. Bright scatterings.
What if ambition is stopping? How immediate
it feels to scent the air.

I came to poetry from two other disciplines—a career as a visual artist and volunteer work as a radio host and producer for my local public radio station. For 15 years, I offered a program called "Audio Saucepan" that combined jazz and world music with readings of contemporary poems. Part of what I love in jazz is how it is held in the improvisations and collaboration, balanced with places of lyrical, rhythmic beauty. In both art and audio mediums, I was interested in blending or reconfiguring. When I started to write poetry in earnest, I folded what I had learned—sound, pattern, texture, composition and segues—into my poems. Gaps in the narrative or description, sometimes shown in fragments, allow me to tighten, change the sonics of the work, and help it leap or shift. There is no static rhythm. I can also combine multiple elements, tenses, time periods and questions together. Although readers may be slightly unnerved by them, I trust that they will find their way.

The second New Mexico Poet Laureate (2022-2025), Lauren Camp is the author of eight books of poetry. A former Astronomer-in-Residence at Grand Canyon National Park, she has received the Dorset Prize and fellowships from the Academy of American Poets and Black Earth Institute. She has been a finalist for the Arab American Book Award, New Mexico-Arizona Book Award, Big Other Book Award, and Adrienne Rich Award. Her poems have been translated into Mandarin, Turkish, Spanish, French, and Arabic. www.laurencamp.com

Marci Calabretta Cancio-Bello

RESTITUTION FOR THE GRANDSON

01-28-2024

If, in the hour of the ox, you had passed
from your own bright life into ours,

or perhaps if your mother had begged
more fervently for you during the spring tide,

when the sea cannot help but give
and give for its fullness,

even if you had not been born
in the ruinous hour of the boar,

as the shore emptied its cupped hands
back into the breakers of neap tide,

if your father had not shut himself up
with the bark and bone of small forests,

had instead cultivated patriarchies
tenderly and fiercely, if and if and yet–

here I stand, lifting my empty net,
slinging into the sea from this precipice

your sister's scrolls, your mother's oath,
the spent cockleshells of clams,

insufficient recompense for what
the sea asks us to return.

Marci Calabretta Cancio-Bello is the author of *Hour of the Ox* (University of Pittsburgh, 2016), which won the AWP Donald Hall Prize and was a finalist for the Milt Kessler Award and Florida Book Award for Poetry. She and E. J. Koh co-translated *The World's Lightest Motorcycle* by Yi Won (Zephyr Press, 2021), which was awarded the Translation Grand Prize from the Literature Translation Institute of Korea. She received a Creative Writing Fellowship in Prose from the National Endowment for the Arts (2022), as well as fellowships from Kundiman, the Knight Foundation, and the American Literary Translators Association, and her work has appeared in the Academy of American Poets, *Catapult, Kenyon Review Online, The New York Times, Poets & Writers, The Rumpus,* and more. In 2021 she co-founded the Adoptee Literary Festival and PEN America Miami/South Florida Chapter. She is a founding member of the Starlings Collective and a program manager for Miami Book Fair.

Kara Candito

A SHORT GENEALOGY OF POWER TOOLS

09-16-2016

There was this shed behind the pre-fab house
      where I straddled a boy named Boomer
on his father's John Deere. Into the shaved back
of his head, I dug my hands to pretend they were
             power tools; my hands blasting
his body open, so I could crawl inside and make it mine.

But afterward, when the mulch smelled feral
      and the wheelbarrow looked like an exhausted animal,
and I had to pee, there was just this total annoyance
with being back in my body, with being a person
         of dumb, particular needs, suddenly
waving hello to his mother, who called
      the bathroom a powder room, which was a sad
suburban lie that cut me anyway.
And the soap was sharp and the shower curtain
was sharp and I was wearing a white sweatshirt.
          And the face in the mirror was the worst

kind of moralist. It said: You cannot invent a thing
      with wires and blades and call it a coronation.
I want to tell you this without saying that my mother's car
was already in the driveway; that shoulder-pads
         and brass buttons made her look like a man;
that when she squinted and said, Stop being so goddamn sullen,
      she was one. And breathing became
this nameless, miraculous crime.

Kara Candito holds an MFA. in creative writing from the University of Maryland, College Park and a PhD in creative writing and literary theory from the Florida State University. She is the author of *Taste of Cherry* (U of Nebraska Press, 2009), winner of the Prairie Schooner Book Prize in Poetry and *Spectator* (U of Utah Press, 2014), and winner of the Agha Shahid Ali Poetry Prize. Her work has appeared in such journals as *AGNI, jubilat, The Kenyon Review, Indiana Review,* and *Drunken Boat.* A recipient of scholarships and awards from the Bread Loaf Writers' Conference, the Council for Wisconsin Writers, the Vermont Studio Center, the MacDowell Colony, and the Santa Fe Arts Institute, Candito is a Creative Writing Professor at the University of Wisconsin-Platteville and a co-curator of the Monsters of Poetry reading series. Her areas of specialization include modernism, Spanish surrealism, and the dramatic monologue (www.karacandito.com).

Cyrus Cassells

THE SHADOW

03-17-2020

after Hans Christian Anderson

Traveler, I came to a colossus
of clustered houses—a sultry kingdom,
replete with breeze-swept balconies,
belled donkeys, and vying boys
slyly triggering Roman candles—
all of it beneath a glittering
caravansary of detectable stars—

In the bullying heat
of that equatorial city,
my rambunctious shadow grew
thinner, desiccated, restless,
and leaped, abracadabra
(more jack-in-the-box
than agile gazelle!),
onto my mysterious neighbor's
intricate balcony.
When my rogue-swift, dark counterpart
returned, I asked:
What did you see? Who lives there?
Poetry, he revealed.
Yes, Poetry, as numinous and longed-for
as the Northern Lights,
often lives in palm-guarded places,
as a shuttered Garbo, an elusive
recluse cloistered among us—

Imagine: I was a seeker tantalized
by light and shadow
that I faithfully mimicked
in expressive oils and aquarelles,
an ardent, itinerant painter, attuned

to the way garden shadows
become diligent brushstrokes
or late afternoon lace.
So why should I be surprised
at my headstrong shadow?

After his first enlightening escapades
in Poetry's captivating rooms,
in one magnanimous gesture,
I set free my shadow to emerge
as his own up-and-coming man,
to acquire blue serge, a boutonniere,
a dapper bowler—
But he employed his newfound humanity,
his effusive charm and flair
to persuade the winsome princess,
my beloved fiancée,
that I was the unruly imposter, the mad
shadow who deserved oblivion:
first bedlam, then the chilly
volley of a firing squad—

And in the flash point I was manacled, I saw
our fierce mirroring was never
friendship, twin-ship,
but a crafty fisherman's net,
a supplanting spider's stratagem—I saw
how slowly and inexorably I became
a Christ in distress,
and my rebellious shadow
a charioteer, a ruffian god,
a key-cold executioner.

Cassells is also the author of *The Mud Actor* (1982), winner of the 1981 National Poetry Series competition; *Soul Make a Path through Shouting* (1994), nominated for the Pulitzer Prize and winner of the William Carlos Williams Award; *Beautiful Signor* (1997), winner of the Lambda Literary Award; *More Than Peace and Cypresses* (2004); *The Crossed-Out Swastika* (2012); and *Is There Room for Another Horse on Your Horse Ranch?* (Four Way Books, 2024). He has received fellowships from the Guggenheim Foundation, the National Endowment for the Arts, and the Rockefeller Foundation. His other honors include the Lannan Literary Award, the Peter I.B. Lavan Younger Poet Award, and two Pushcart Prizes.

Jennifer Chang
THE WINTER'S WIFE

02-25-2019

It will be years before I understand
failure. The sun's last rage
in the winter trees. My yard
is a failure of field. It is small
and poorly tended. Years before
this hard kernel of worry
rises to a truer height, I can learn
to make shade with my palms,
but I cannot learn to unmoor my want.
I want wild roots to prosper
an invention of blooms, each unknown
to every wise gardener. If I could be
a color. If I could be a question
of tender regard. I know crabgrass
and thistle. I know one algorithm:
it has nothing to do with repetition
or rhythm. It is the route from number
to number (less to more, more
to less), a map drawn by proof,
not faith. Unlike twilight, I do not
conclude with darkness. I conclude.

Jennifer Chang is the author of *The History of Anonymity*, *Some Say the Lark*, and *An Authentic Life*. Her work has been honored with fellowships from MacDowell, Yaddo, and the Elizabeth Murray Artists Residency and with the William Carlos Williams Award, a Pushcart Prize, and the Levinson Prize from *Poetry* magazine. She teaches at the University of Texas in Austin and is the poetry editor of *New England Review*.

Grant Clauser

LUCKY

4-7-2020

He remembers pushing the knife
deep behind the jaw
and cutting down to its tail.
If he was good he could wrap
his pointing finger around the guts
at the gill and pull them all out
in one feather like when his mother
waved at the driveway
and said father won't be back
or anything tonight
then went to her room
and shut herself for three days
until someone called the neighbor.
He remembers thinking that raccoons
must be so lucky
to find those fish guts laying
in the weeds
like a man who finds
his shotgun fully loaded
and everyone asleep.

We receive messages about violence every day in media. TV and movies glorify or fetishize it. The news leads with it. World leaders bargain with it. And individuals and families live with it every day. If violence is part of the human experience, it's also part of the poetry experience. There's violence in the Aeneid, in Shakespeare, in Frank Stanford. This particular poem doesn't describe an event that happened, but it does capture some of the feelings and tensions from a couple of people I knew as a kid. It's a conglomeration enhanced with imagination. Poetry is always the right place to examine the things we don't want to face out in the open. Poetry won't provide any answers, but it may offer multiple ways to look at it and, maybe, to cope.

Grant Clauser has published five poetry collections: *Muddy Dragon on the Road to Heaven*, Winner of the Codhill Press Poetry Award; *Reckless Constellations*, winner of the *Cider Press Review* Editor's Award; *The Magician's Handbook*; *Necessary Myths*, winner of Dogfish Head Poetry prize; and *The Trouble with Rivers*. In 2014 he was a guest poet of the Sharjah International Book Fair in the United Arab Emirates. He's also a founding member of the poetry improv group No River Twice. His favorite dry fly is the Parachute Adams. His favorite nymph is a basic Hare's Ear with a brass bead. For bass he sticks mostly to a Clouser Minnow (no relation) and sometimes a Murry Hellgrammite.

Kai Coggin

THE FIRST KISS I DON'T COUNT

03-03-2021

it's one I've never
written about
don't count
or even consider legitimate
there were no
shooting stars
weak knees
or butterflies
his mouth
a stranger
dark
the taste of metal
blood maybe
sweat
smoke of swisher sweets

13
is an in between state
consciousness of a woman-too-soon
in the body
of a child
and
he was a stranger
who knocked on the door
and asked for a glass of water
and it was hot and it was July
and I let him inside
the house
his skin glistened like a night of stars
we sat on the couch
his name was Leroy
and he put my hands around
his hard flesh
and Gilligan's Island was on TV
skipper the professor too
and see
it's funny what memories do

43

remembers these flashes
but I can still taste
the mouth
of a stranger
and I tried to wash
the
blood
off my Winnie the Pooh bedsheets
and I ran the bathwater
over
my thighs
and something
something was broken
and it was hot and it was July

and I did not have a name for this
  other
      than
         SIN

and I did not have a name for this
but this would be a silence
that would hold my tongue for years

and I don't really ever count it
as my first kiss
because so much more was taken
and he was a stranger
and it was hot and it was July
and Gilligan's Island was on TV

and I could not
stop crying
I just could not stop crying

the

bathwater

muffling

my loss

Kai Coggin (she/her) is the inaugural Poet Laureate of the City of Hot Springs, AR and a recipient of a 2024 Academy of American Poets Laureate Fellowship for her project Sharing Tree Space. She is the author of five collections, most recently *Mother of Other Kingdoms* (Harbor Editions, 2024) and *Mining for Stardust* (FlowerSong Press 2021). Coggin is a Certified Master Naturalist, a K-12 Teaching Artist in poetry with the Arkansas Arts Council, an Interchange Grant Fellow with the Mid-America Arts Alliance, and host of the longest running consecutive weekly open mic series in the country—Wednesday Night Poetry.

Aaron Coleman

VESTIGIA

11-26-2018

The trees teach me how to break and keep on living. Patience
and nuance and another kind of strength. That kind of life
wrought from water and mineral iron and loss, the perpetual loss
that emanates from underneath tongues, leaves. The hush splayed
across the jungle made of memory. More fearful for its lack
of movement. The sad lusciousness our eyes reason from a world
on pause. Motionless green. What we touch and see, immediate
as steam, then gone, collected. Tense, wet beads full of secrets; how
to make a branch long. Nothing swaying the weight of the trees.

Aaron Coleman is a poet, translator, and scholar of the African diaspora. He is
the author of Red Wilderness (Four Way Books, 2025), among other titles, and the
translator of Nicolás Guillén's The Great Zoo (University of Chicago Press, 2024),
short-listed for the 2025 Griffin Poetry Prize. The recipient of support from Cave
Canem and the National Endowment for the Arts, Coleman is the postdoctoral
fellow in critical translation studies at the University of Michigan.

Nicole Cooley

ROMANCE

04-05-09

On the train to New Orleans my sister and I
light the Virgen de Guadalupe candles
and the line of unlucky women steps out from the flame.

They file past at the window where we sit,
where we have given up being safe from them,
our four aunts with their loose dresses for mourning,

their fasting, their silent refusals. These women loved
their grief like the bread they would not let themselves eat,
like the children they would not allow into their bodies.

We know their unspoken lesson—take nothing
into the body. We know they will wait for us,
a line of dolls cut from the same sheet of butcher paper,

the sister of this family linked by their hands and alone.
One mile into Mississippi, the train passes a statue
of blue-robed Mary in someone else's yard, bathtubs leaning

against the wire fence. I place us there. With relief,
I lower each of us into the bath, into the crystal salts.
Oil pools on the surface of the water. Sulfur is staining our skin.

The train drags on across the tracks, away from us,
leaving us in our own story. My first aunt looks down
at the flat pan of her pelvis, strung tight between hipbones

she'll never touch. She likes her body empty and clean.
Coaxing her into the tub, we preach the virtues of this water,
its power to wash away sin. The second one taps

her cigarette ash on the grass and blows smoke at the sky
while we plead with her about drowning,

47

tell her not to go all the way down. Why should she listen?

We know how good the body can feel, unused, expecting
nothing. But my sister and I are trying to prove them wrong.
When I kneel beside my family, I am desperate.

My sister drags the sign of the cross in the dirt
with a stick. Why don't we quit telling the story?
Once upon a time there were four princesses and a single

safe tower. No prince. In place of a man, a basket
of primroses they ripped into pieces, four finches
fighting it out for the kingdom. In another story,

my sister and I take them all home to New Orleans.
I take them all into me, my secret collection.
I give up. They live in my body. Oh, we are beautiful.

In the real story, we are all starving together. Sisters,
the wafer floats on my tongue like bad luck, like our name.

Poems should entertain, frighten, please, flatter, make us rethink and reframe, save the world, even. Because that is what's true to the human experience. I like a poetry that, to paraphrase Whitman, can "contain multitudes." Still, one of my writing teachers at Iowa said, "If you have writers block, lower your standards." Hearing that was incredibly helpful. I realized that while I may not be capable of writing a good poem on a given day, I can write a bad one—which then of course might become something Whitman would claims contains those multitudes. I love telling my students this quote. They often look aghast.

Nicole Cooley grew up in New Orleans, Louisiana. Her most recent book is the collection of poetry *Mother Water Ash* (Louisiana University Press, July 2024) as well as the two poetry collections, *Girl after Girl after Girl* (Louisiana State University Press, 2017) and *Of Marriage* (Alice James Books, 2018). She has published four other collections of poems, *Breach, Milk Dress, The Afflicted Girls* and *Resurrection*, as well as a novel, *Judy Garland, Ginger Love*, two chapbooks, *Frozen Charlottes, A Sequence*, and *Vanishing Point*, and a collaborative artists' book (with book artist Maureen Cummins), *Salem Lessons*.

Steve Davenport

ARRANGE THEIR SEA-SMOOTH BONES IN FOURTEEN BROKEN ROWS

03-29-2010

In your lizard-skin boots, reread the book of myths.
Dip it two parts whiskey to one part gunpowder.
Fall in tongues or fever, thieving the terrible.
Wake and feel the fell of dark, not day. What black hours.
Then saddle a sea horse and dive into the wreck.
Salvage all you can of the poets buried there.
Arrange their sea-smooth bones in fourteen broken rows.
Art is entrails spilled and a hand drawing itself.
Decide on a syllable count of twelve per line.
Carve out your space as the Cowgirl of Amour Fou
or the Cowboy of Ra rocking the Drunken Boat.
Employ a figure, a sidekick, to kick your ass.
Call him Murfy and take his advice: sonnetry
like shrapnel, like bricks through the living room window.

A product of American Bottom, the Illinois floodplain across the Mississippi from St. Louis, Steve Davenport is the author of three poetry collections: *Bruise Songs* (2020), *Overpass* (2012) and *Uncontainable Noise* (2006). His poems, stories, and essays have been anthologized, reprinted, and published in scores of literary magazines both on-line and in print. A story in *The Southern Review* received a 2011 Pushcart Prize Special Mention. His *Murder on Gasoline Lake*, published in *Black Warrior Review* and later as a chapbook, is listed as Notable in *Best American Essays 2007*. He lives in Urbana, Illinois.

Todd Davis

LAST OF DECEMBER

11-01-2010

Cottonwood flames, cherry parallels fire—
out of the crack and hinge, quiet whistle
over the grate: a comfort to know the dead sing
even as they pass into the new year.

Todd Davis is the author of eight full-length collections of poetry—*Ditch Memory: New & Selected Poems*, *Coffin Honey*, *Native Species*, *Winterkill*, *In the Kingdom of the Ditch*, *The Least of These*, *Some Heaven*, and *Ripe*—as well as of a limited edition chapbook, *Household of Water, Moon, and Snow*. He edited the nonfiction collection, *Fast Break to Line Break: Poets on the Art of Basketball*, and co-edited *A Literary Field Guide to Northern Appalachia* and *Making Poems: Forty Poems with Commentary by the Poets*. His poetry has appeared in Ted Kooser's syndicated newspaper column *American Life in Poetry* and has been anthologized in such books as *The Autumn House Anthology of Contemporary American Poetry* and Bedford/St. Martin's textbook, *Approaching Literature*. His poems have won the Gwendolyn Brooks Poetry Prize, the Chautauqua Editor's Prize, the Midwest Book Award, the ForeWord INDIES Book of the Year Bronze and Silver Awards, and the Bloomsburg University Book Prize. More than 400 of his poems have appeared in such noted journals and magazines as *American Poetry Review*, *Iowa Review*, *Ecotone*, *North American Review*, *Indiana Review*, *Alaska Quarterly Review*, *Iowa Review*, *Missouri Review*, *Poetry Northwest*, *Gettysburg Review*, *Orion*, *West Branch*, *Southern Humanities Review*, and *Poetry Daily*. He teaches creative writing, American literature, and environmental studies at Pennsylvania State University's Altoona College.

Linda Bryant Davis

DIGEST OF RED

10-18-2023

Got married in red
velvet. Not bright like a clown
nose but like blackened
cherry, old blood. Grandma
warned: Marry in red, you're better
off dead. At birth

my baby breathed 30 fragments
of air & like teakettle
steam vanished. Cheap
apartment carpet red. Tattered
theater curtains in two tones
of claret. Red like rust

nibbling the old Blazer. Mom
delighted in the streaks
of cardinal flitting in the hospice
courtyard through the bending
willows. I remember her last
hours, how she stared

at the sunset before the morphine
trance. I was in the electric
shock of divorce. Red hues
comforted me. I said yes
to crawdads in the shiny
vat, to the eruption of flame

maple & beetroot. Lucky
as a cornsnake who sheds
her vermilion skindress, I stake
my claim. I breathe. I am
not Plath. Not Sexton
or Woolf. I stumble still

into mudslides of heavy
heartedness. I gather
myself like a disheveled
bouquet, red
tinged petals
tumbling.

Linda Bryant (Davis) is a retired journalist who is now dedicated to writing with more creativity and imagination than her career required. She lives in Berea, Kentucky and owns Owsley Fork Writers Sanctuary.

Tyree Daye

LORD HERE

01-17-2018

I learned what a bullet does to a back, to a mother.

After every funeral it rains,

      I was told that's God crying in Youngsville.

My uncle walked our holed streets

      until he died sun-soaked, broken in,

left me young boy and bitter in Youngsville.

Hallelujahs knocked on screen doors,

        let the lord in.

      We stood on porches and watched the saved

stitch wings in Youngsville.

Black berries hung in my aunt's back yard where we cut

      the asshole off a trout,

guts laid on a cutting board in Youngsville.

We were told a storm was a sermon,

      lightning horse whips the sky,

milks rain in Youngsville.

Tyree Daye was raised in Youngsville, North Carolina. He is the author of the poetry collections a little bump in the earth (Copper Canyon Press, 2024); Cardinal (Copper Canyon Press, 2020); and River Hymns (American Poetry Review, 2017), the winner of the APR/Honickman First Book Prize.

Linh Dinh

BORDERLESS BODY

02-07-2018

Before, I was a miserly person, dried up, stiff,
Stuck, completely wrung, stuttering, fanatical,

But this morning, my skin felt unusually cool and conscious.
My body tingled. Suddenly I could understand and speak

2,000 languages. My soul blossomed, my breasts budded.
I peeled back my foreskin to scrape clean all of my obsolete

And labored presumptions. My teeth, the gaps in between
My teeth and my breath felt unusually fresh and clean.

I could see very far away. I could sympathize with each
Strand of hair stranded on the skin of each person.

Shuddering, I ejaculated for the first time in life, into life.
I became aware of my miraculous vagina and anus.

Finally, I had been allowed to spread out, to blend into
All humans, animals and things. I just wanted to leap up

To kiss everyone right away. I just wanted to service
And suck everyone right away. I also wanted to be sucked

By everyone on this earth. I was willing to forgive
And apologize to each toe joint on each person.

Naked, I walk through the street as the very first human.

Born in Vietnam in 1963, I lived mostly in the US from 1975 until 2018, but have returned to Vietnam. I'm the author of a non-fiction book, *Postcards from the End of America* (2017), a novel, *Love Like Hate* (2010), two books of stories, *Fake House* (2000) and *Blood and Soap* (2004), and six collections of poems. I've been anthologized in *Best American Poetry 2000, 2004, 2007, Great American Prose Poems from Poe to the Present, Postmodern American Poetry: a Norton Anthology* (vol. 2) and flash fiction International: *Very Short Stories from Around the World*, etc. I'm also editor of *Night, Again: Contemporary Fiction from Vietnam* (1996) and *The Deluge: New Vietnamese Poetry* (2013). My writing has been translated into Japanese, Italian, Spanish, French, Dutch, German, Portuguese, Korean, Arabic, Icelandic, Serbian and Finnish. I've also published widely in Vietnamese.

Camille Dungy

A MASSIVE DYING OFF

12-23-2014

When the fish began their dying you didn't worry.

You bought new shoes.
            They looked like crocodiles:
snappy and rich,
        brown as delta mud.

                Even the box they shipped in was beautiful, bejeweled.

You tore through masses of swaddling paper,
        these shoes!

        carefully cradled
in all that cardboard by what
                you now understand
must have been someone's tiny, indifferent hands.

    *

The five-fingered sea stars you heard about on NPR.

You must have been driving to Costco.
It must have been before all the visitors arrived.

You needed covers, pillows, disposable containers.
At Costco, everything comes cheap.

Sea stars, jellies, anemones, all the scuttlers and hoverers
and clingers along the ocean floor. A massive dying off, further displacing
depleted oxygen, cried the radio announcer.

You plugged in your iPod.
Enough talk. You'd found the song you had been searching for.

*

One cargo ship going out. One cargo ship coming in.

                              Crabs crawling up trawler lines.
                                Giant lobsters walking
                                        right onto the shore.

                You've been sitting in your car
            watching the sunset over the Golden Gate.
                        NPR again.

One cargo ship going out. One cargo ship coming in.

                              Those who can are leaving.

        The Marin Headlands crouch
toward the ocean,
            fog so thick on their side of the bay
                    you can't tell crag from cloud from sea.

One cargo ship headed out, another coming in.

                        They're looking for a place
                            where they can breath.

                You've been here less than an hour.
When the sun has finished setting
you'll go home.

*

In the dream, your father is the last refuse to wash ashore.
                    This wasn't what you wanted.
                            Any of you.
                                    The first sign

of trouble was the bottle with the message.
        That washed up years ago.
Then, so many bottles
                the stenographers couldn't answer all the messages anymore.

The women of the village wept when your father died.

Then they lined up to deliver tear-stained tissue to the secretary of the interior
    who translated their meaning
and had it writ out on a scroll.

These were the answers your people had been waiting for!

        That papyrus wound around your father like a bandage.
    The occasion announced,
        you prayed proper prayers, loaded him onto an outrigger,
set him off,
           but here he is again. Stinking.
    Swelling.

You can't dispose of the rising dead and you're worried.
    What can you do?

I am rarely, more likely never, reaching for a statement in poetry. That I might arrive at a statement in poetry upon the successful completion of a poem is fine with me. But if I am reaching at the outset of a poem for a statement I am significantly more likely to create propaganda than poetry.

Camille T. Dungy was born and raised in the western United States (Colorado and California), though she has lived briefly in most other regions of the U.S. and has spent time on all but one continent and several countries. Dungy attributes some of the energy in her writing to both her delight in going new places and meeting new people and the good fortune of having a beautiful place to root down and call home. In much of her writing, Dungy considers history, landscape, culture, family, and desire. Her latest book, *Soil: The Story of a Black Mother's Garden* was published by Simon and Schuster in 2023. Dungy is also the author of four collections of poetry, most recently *Trophic Cascade* (Wesleyan UP 2017), winner of the Colorado Book Award, and a *Guidebook to Relative Strangers: Journeys into Race, Motherhood, and History* (W.W. Norton &Co: 2017), which was a finalist for the National Book Critics Circle Award in criticism.

Martín Espada

FLOATERS

02-09-2021

*Ok, I'm gonna go ahead and ask…have ya'll ever seen floaters this
clean. I'm not trying to be an a$$ but I HAVE NEVER SEEN
FLOATERS LIKE THIS, could this be another edited photo. We've all
seen the dems and liberal parties do some pretty sick things.*
—Anonymous post, "I'm 10-15" Border Patrol Facebook group

Like a beer bottle thrown into the river by a boy too drunk to cry,
like the shard of a Styrofoam cup drained of coffee brown as the river,
like the plank of a fishing boat broken in half by the river, the dead float.
And the dead have a name: *floaters*, say the men of the Border Patrol,
keeping watch all night by the river, hearts pumping coffee as they say
the word *floaters*, soft as a bubble, hard as a shoe as it nudges the body,
to see if it breathes, to see if it moans, to see if it sits up and speaks.

And the dead have names, a feast day parade of names, names that
dress all in red, names that twirl skirts, names that blow whistles,
names that shake rattles, names that sing in praise of the saints:
Say *Óscar Alberto Martínez Ramírez*. Say *Angie Valeria Martínez Ávalos*.
See how they rise off the tongue, the calling of bird to bird somewhere
in the trees above our heads, trilling in the dark heart of the leaves.

Say what we know of them now they are dead: Óscar slapped dough
for pizza with oven-blistered fingers. Daughter Valeria sang, banging
a toy guitar. He slipped free of the apron he wore in the blast of the oven,
sold the motorcycle he would kick till it sputtered to life, counted off
pesos for the journey across the river, and the last of his twenty-five
years, and the last of her twenty-three months. There is another name
that beats its wings in the heart of the trees: *Say Tania Vanessa Ávalos*,
Óscar's wife and Valeria's mother, the witness stumbling along the river.

Now their names rise off her tongue: Say *Óscar y Valeria*. He swam
from Matamoros across to Brownsville, the girl slung around his neck,
stood her in the weeds on the Texas side of the river, swore to return
with her mother in hand, turning his back as fathers do who later say:
I turned around and she was gone. In the time it takes for a bird to hop
from branch to branch, Valeria jumped in the river after her father.

59

Maybe he called out her name as he swept her up from the river;
maybe the river drowned out his voice as the water swept them away.
Tania called out the names of the saints, but the saints drowsed
in the stupor of birds in the dark, their cages covered with blankets.
The men on patrol would never hear their pleas for asylum, watching
for *floaters*, hearts pumping coffee all night on the Texas side of the river.

No one, they say, had ever seen *floaters this clean*: Óscar's black shirt
yanked up to the armpits, Valeria's arm slung around her father's
neck even after the light left her eyes, both face down in the weeds,
back on the Mexican side of the river. *Another edited photo*: See how
her head disappears in his shirt, the waterlogged diaper bunched
in her pants, the blue of the blue cans. The radio warned us about
the *crisis actors* we see at one school shooting after another; the man
called *Óscar* will breathe, sit up, speak, tug the black shirt over
his head, shower off the mud and shake hands with the photographer.

Yet, the floaters did not float down the Río Grande like Olympians
showing off the backstroke, nor did their souls float up to Dallas,
land of rumored jobs and a president shot in the head as he waved
from his motorcade. No bubbles rose from their breath in the mud,
light as the iridescent circles of soap that would fascinate a two-year old.

And the dead still have names, names that sing in praise of the saints,
names that flower in blossoms of white, a cortege of names dressed
all in black, trailing the coffins to the cemetery. Carve their names
in headlines and gravestones they would never know in the kitchens
of this cacophonous world. Enter their names in the book of names.
Say *Óscar Alberto Martínez Ramírez*; say *Angie Valeria Martínez Ávalos*.
Bury them in a corner of the cemetery named for the sainted archbishop
of the poor, shot in the heart saying mass, bullets bought by the taxes
I paid when I worked as a bouncer and fractured my hand forty years
ago, and bumper stickers read: *El Salvador is Spanish for Vietnam*.

When the last bubble of breath escapes the body, may the men
who speak of floaters, who have never seen floaters this clean,
float through the clouds to the heavens, where they paddle the air
as they wait for the saint who flips through the keys on his ring
like a drowsy janitor, till he fingers the key that turns the lock and shuts
the gate on their babble-tongued faces, and they plunge back to earth,
a shower of hailstones pelting the river, the Mexican side of the river.

Martín Espada has published more than twenty books as a poet, editor, essayist, and translator. His new book of poems is called *Jailbreak of Sparrows*. His previous book, *Floaters*, won the National Book Award for Poetry in 2021. Other poetry collections include *Vivas to Those Who Have Failed* (2016), *The Trouble Ball* (2011), *The Republic of Poetry* (2006), *Alabanza* (2003) and *Imagine the Angels of Bread* (1996). He is the editor of *What Saves Us: Poems of Empathy and Outrage in the Age of Trump* (2019). Espada has received the Ruth Lilly Poetry Prize, the Shelley Memorial Award, the Robert Creeley Award, an Academy of American Poets Fellowship, the PEN/Revson Fellowship, a Letras Boricuas Fellowship, and a Guggenheim Fellowship. The title poem of his collection *Alabanza*, about 9/11, has been widely anthologized and performed. His book of essays and poems, *Zapata's Disciple* (1998), was banned in Tucson as part of the Mexican-American Studies Program outlawed by the state of Arizona. A former tenant lawyer with Su Clínica Legal in Greater Boston, Espada is a professor of English at the University of Massachusetts-Amherst.

Blas Falconer

A LOVE POEM

01-22-2019

I fell asleep to the sound of water moving in the dark.

In the morning, the river, what was left of the snow, filled the window in my hotel room, rushing faster than I'd imagined.

To be here, among the foothills, and not there was like wanting, all at once, to hold the same stone in each hand.

And all at once, there was a center where there hadn't been, the way there seems a center in a field where crows roost in winter.

Call it clarity, or the footing a fisherman finds on the bank, whipping his line in the air above his head.

What I wanted was not possible: After the birds have gone, the great nests of leaves and limbs high among leaves and limbs.

He catches the fish he's wanted all day, pulls the hook from its mouth, and lets it go.

Which I must remember and remember to tell you.

When I was writing my first collection, I gravitated toward ten-syllable lines to evoke a conversational tone. I liked how slight shifts in lineation could subtly change the music or emotional pitch. But when I began my second book, the poems sounded too much like the first—so I started experimenting with prose poems. At first, those prose blocks felt inert. But I discovered that syntax and the poetic leap could do some of the work that lineation had

done before. Paragraph breaks, I hoped, would offer just enough pause to help readers make those leaps with me. Over time, I became more attuned to the breath of a sentence—the way a long sentence can stretch toward its breaking point and then release. That breathlessness became a kind of form: the long, single-line stanza. I stopped thinking of them as prose poems and began seeing them as lines and stanzas in their own right—just unusually extended ones. This form changed the poems. It invited a more meditative mode, one that tracked the mind in motion rather than unfolding a narrative scene. I found myself chasing clarity, but not conclusion—turns of thought rather than plot, a different syntax, a different music.

Blas Falconer is the author of *Rara Avis* (Four Way Books 2024); *Forgive the Body This Failure* (Four Way Books, 2018); *The Foundling Wheel* (Four Way Books, 2012); *A Question of Gravity and Light* (University of Arizona Press, 2007); and *The Perfect Hour* (Pleasure Boat Studio: A Literary Press, 2006). He is also a co-editor for *The Other Latin@: Writing Against a Singular Identity* (University of Arizona Press, 2011) and *Mentor & Muse: Essays from Poets to Poets* (Southern Illinois University Press, 2010).

Nick Flynn

BAG OF MICE

10-04-2010

I dreamt your suicide note
was scrawled in pencil on a brown paperbag,
& in the bag were six baby mice. The bag
opened into darkness,
smoldering
from the top down. The mice,
huddled at the bottom, scurried the bag
across a shorn field. I stood over it
& as the burning reached each carbon letter
of what you'd written
your voice released into the night
like a song, & the mice
grew wilder.

Nick Flynn (writer, playwright, and poet) is the author of thirteen books, including *Low* (Graywolf, 2023) and *Some Ether* (Graywolf, 2000), winner of the PEN/Joyce Osterweil Award. His bestselling memoir *Another Bullshit Night in Suck City* (Norton, 2004) was made into a film starring Robert DeNiro (focus features, 2012) and has been translated into fifteen languages. *Stay: Threads, Collaborations, and Conversations* (Ze Books, 2020), documents twenty-five years of his collaborations with artists, filmmakers, and composers.

CMarie Fuhrman

CAMPED BENEATH THE DAM

03-03-2020

Camped beneath Hells Canyon Dam
last night it started raining.
I moved my head outside the tent and let
rain fill the hollows of my eyes.

I never saw lightning
but heard thunder roll from beneath me,
the earth upside down, hooves of animals
bolting through clouds.
It started raining lamprey and sturgeon.

It rained so hard last night I was young again.
It rained so hard the earth moved
from the graves of my grandparents.
Their bones started dancing on the rocks
dancing like hail.

It rained so hard the river was young again.
Neither of us had our second names.
We chewed dirt with our first teeth.
We ran together with salmon, steelhead,
the shores lifted their skirts at our passing.

Last night the rain brought back my grandmother.
She put my head in her lap.
She told me stories, she told me carp
sucked the bones of my grandfather
her tears filled my eyes. Her braids tickled
my cheeks.

This morning the skies are clear. A fly dances
on my nose. In the flooding light I move earth
worms from the trail. Sometimes
I toss their wet red bodies back into the river.

CMarie Fuhrman is an author and poet whose work is rooted in the landscape of the West. She has authored a book of essays, *Salmon Weather* and *Camped Beneath the Dam: Poems*. She has also co-edited two significant anthologies, *Cascadia Field Guide: Art, Ecology, and Poetry* and *Native Voices: Indigenous Poetry, Craft, and Conversations*. She hosts Terra Firma, a podcast from Colorado Public Radio, and has published or forthcoming poetry and nonfiction in multiple journals, including *Terrain.org*, *Emergence Magazine*, *Platform Review*, *Northwest Review*, *Yellow Medicine Review*, *Poetry Northwest*, and several anthologies. CMarie is an award-winning columnist for the *Inlander*, a former Idaho Writer in Residence, and the Elk River Writers Workshop Director. She is the Assistant Director for the Graduate Program in Creative Writing at Western Colorado University, where she teaches Nature Writing. CMarie resides in the Salmon River Mountains of Idaho.

Ross Gay

NURSERY

11-29-2012

this little one's snout in the bones
this little one's snout
in the bones with its tongue
out this little one's
moan the spine
of the night this one's
ruddy cock made stiff by the screams
this one wet-faced this little one
with a face like a boy's this
one shriveled to the size of a rat
its eyes replaced with flies that
one's mother with her teats
dried up snapping
at the flies in her little one's eyes
this little one with its snout draws a circle
in the dirt around his dead
and dying this one with gristle
in his teeth pisses in the circle
where the dead lay dying
this little one snatches
food from the sick
and drops it at the fat
one's feet who
waddles when he walks
who opens his
mouth to excrete this
little one's teeth glint
in the rain this one's
eyes stay locked this
one's ears bend
to the pain this little one chews
on rocks this one drags
by their necks the old
and weak to

the holes he's dug
and fills the open graves
of their mouths
with mud this little one
snaps birds from the air
chewing their wings
and flight this one
gnaws its tongue this
one eats the lice
this little one sat curled
in a lump pretending
he was dead that little
one curled up
in a hole and couldn't
quiet her head
these little ones crawling
from their holes to
study the patterns of the bones
spilled and splayed and
broke as a language
as a king on fire in
his home the little ones crawling
from their holes to read
the story of the bones
to set the king on fire
in his home

BIO: Joy.

Hollay Ghadery

REBELLION BOX

09-08-2025
(Fort Henry, Kingston, 1837)

Ask your husband about the honey bees. I may
have an affinity for things that drone and drown
out. On the way here everything was so green, it hurt
the trees practically threw themselves on the road
and to think, only days ago I'd been worried about
my nose most of all. Now, John's been hung and the rest

of us rot and cut away at stove wood. Just rest
and fleas for the foolish. I know some of us may
have stepped into battle thinking only about
valour, liberty, winning. It's easy to drown
in these abstracts but it's a dangerous road
to follow. I've seen how brave men hurt

so easily. Tell Mary I think of her often. It can hurt
to think of myself like this: all stone and soot, but rest
assured my present circumstance is not finite. Every road
leads home. It's true, our troops sat in that tavern and may
have felt some degree of foreboding already. We drown
our fear, glass after glass. I admit I was afraid to think about

Mary. Home. Honey bees and my broken nose, about
to fall off my face from want of attention. I know I hurt
the most remarkable people. God, Mary. I will drown
my primitive conditions. I've managed to create. I rest
in dirt and root myself to the root of her. I may
be the most pressing of hopeless things, because road

after road and I still brandish youth like a shotgun. Road
after road leads to finding something to do about
all this time on my hands. I dovetail my work. I may
be the most diligent of craftsmen. All this time can hurt,
weigh black and blue in the middle of my face, the rest

69

—the luxury of a blue cotton dress—the rest can drown

like marzipan creek pebbles, July's sweetgrass chew. Drown,
and wait, because all that talk and rallying—it cleared a road.
I won't stand for futility. There are so many reasons to rest
your beliefs here, and not one of us has. I write home about
paying debts on time, mending the fence. I write to avoid hurt,
boredom—being forgotten. I write you about the bees. You may

remember the summer we cleared your husband's land. May
came hard and the bees came early. I was stung twice. It hurt,
but Mary was in blue, and it was something else to think about.

Hollay Ghadery is a multi-genre writer living in rural Ontario on Anishinaabe land.
She has her MFA in Creative Writing from the University of Guelph and her poetry,
short stories, and personal essays have appeared in literary journals and magazines
around the world, including *The Malahat Review*, and *The Fiddlehead*.

Aracelis Girmay

THE BLACK MARIA

I.

-after Neil deGrasse Tyson, black astrophysicist & director of the Hayden Planetarium, born in 1958, New York City. In his youth, deGrasse Tyson was confronted by police on more than one occasion when he was on his way to study stars.

"I've known that I've wanted to do astrophysics since I was nine years old, a first visit to the Hayden Planetarium...

So I got to see how the world around me reacted to my expression of these ambitions. & all I can say is, the fact that I wanted to be a scientist, an astrophysicist, was, hands down, the path of most resistance... Anytime I expressed this interest teachers would say, Don't you want to be an athlete? Or, Don't you wanna... I wanted to become something that was outside of the paradigms of expectation of the people in power.

And I look behind me and say, Well, where are the others who might have been this? And they're not there. And I wonder, What is the [thing] along the tracks that I happened to survive and others did not? Simply because of the forces that prevented it. At every turn. At every turn." –NdT, The Center for Inquiry, 2007

> *Body of space. Body of dark.*
> *Body of light.*

The Skyview apartments
circa 1973, a boy is
kneeling on the rooftop, a boy who
(it is important
to mention here his skin
is brown) prepares his telescope,
the weights & rods,
to better see the moon. His neighbor

71

(it is important to mention here
that she is white) calls the police
because she suspects the brown boy
of something, she does not know
what at first, then turns,
with her white looking,
his telescope into a gun,
his duffel into a bag of objects
thieved from the neighbors' houses
(maybe even hers) & the police
(it is important to mention
that statistically they
are also white) arrive to find
the boy who has been turned, by now,
into "the suspect," on the roof
with a long, black lens, which is,
in the neighbor's mind, a weapon &
depending on who you are, reading this,
you know that the boy is in grave danger,
& you might have known
somewhere quiet in your gut,
you might have worried for him
in the white space between lines 5 & 6,
or maybe even earlier, & you might be holding
your breath for him right now
because you know this story,
it's a true story, though,
miraculously, in this version
of the story anyway,
the boy on the roof of the Skyview lives
to tell the police that he is studying
the night & moon & lives
long enough to offer them (the cops) a view
through his telescope's long, black eye, which,
if I am spelling it out anyway,
is the instrument he borrowed
& the beautiful "trouble" he went through
lugging it up to the roof
to better see the leopard body of
space speckled with stars & the moon far off,
much farther than (since I am spelling *The Thing*

out) the distance between
the white neighbor who cannot see the boy
who is her neighbor, who,
in fact, is much nearer
to her than to the moon, the boy who
wants to understand the large
& gloriously un-human mysteries of
the galaxy, the boy who, despite "America,"
has not been killed by the murderous jury of
his neighbor's imagination & wound. This poem
wants only the moon in its hair & the boy on the roof.
This boy on the roof of this poem
with a moon in his heart. Inside my own body
as I write this poem my body
is making a boy even as the radio
calls out the Missouri coroner's news,
the Ohio coroner's news.
2015. My boy will nod
for his milk & close his mouth around
the black eye of my nipple.
We will survive. How did it happen?
The boy. The cops. My body in this poem.
My milk pulling down into droplets of light
as the baby drinks & drinks them down
into the body that is his own, see it,
splayed & sighing as a star in my arms.
Maybe he will be the boy who studies stars.
Maybe he will be (say it)
the boy on the coroner's table
splayed & spangled
by an officer's lead as if he, too, weren't made
of a trillion glorious cells & sentences. Trying to last.

Leadless, remember? The body's beginning,
splendored with breaths, turned,
by time, into, at least, this song.
This moment-made & the mackerel-"soul"
caught flashing inside the brief moment of the body's net,
then, whoosh, back into the sea of space.

The poem dreams of bodies always leadless, bearing
only things ordinary
as water & light.

Aracelis Girmay is a poet who makes works across genres. She is the author of the poetry collections *the black maria* (BOA, 2016), *Kingdom Animalia* (BOA, 2011), and *Teeth* (Curbstone, 2007). For this work she was a finalist for the Neustadt International Prize for Literature. Her books have also been named finalists for the National Book Critics Circle Award, the Hurston/Wright Legacy Award, and the Connecticut Book Award. She has received fellowships from the Whiting Foundation, Civitella Ranieri, the National Endowment for the Arts, and the Cave Canem Foundation, among others. Girmay is the author of the forthcoming chapbook, *and was a flower*, made in collaboration with book artist Valentina Améstica. Other recent work includes a picture book collaboration with her sister entitled *What Do You Know?* and the forthcoming picture book collaboration with artist Diana Ejaita entitled *Kamau and Zuzu Find A Way*, both with Enchanted Lion Books. Recent works (poetry and prose) have been published or are forthcoming in *Astra*, *The Paris Review* online, *Periphery Journal*, *Jewish Currents*, *The New York Times Magazine*, and *e-flux*.

Eugene Gloria

SAINT JOE

02-04-2013

after James Wright

When the choppers churned and swayed
the swift brown current like a field of cogon grasses,
we dropped a rope below,
but the native girl, no older than my daughter,
was too weak to hold on, and let go.
We had to leave her to refuel, though we knew
what the river would do. When my duty was up,
I chose to come here, for humid sheets over bamboo beds,
for some honey in a slip—
a ninety-pound rice cooker named Ronda
and the soap dance she's known to do. But hardly for love,
as I wait with this man bent in my arms.
When the Coca-Cola truck hit this pedicab driver,
you could see his rubber slippers fly
all the way up to the second-floor window.
His body thrown five meters from his cab.
I imagine the Lord Jesus descending from his cross,
a good marine saving the dead in limbo.
But on this god-forgotten street a crowd gathers,
crows peck and gawk, and name me "Joe."
Their faces tell a separate story, each one
ending with the sweet by-and-by, like the girl
whose hands slipped at the end of my rope
dancing above the fury of a bloated river.
A man in a suit slouches off, whistles for a cab;
a flotilla of rubber slippers converges on a two-inch lake of rain.
A pair of white hands, mine, reach for his limp body.
And from the swollen streets, an ambulance calls,
draws closer, louder. And I hold on,
listen to children chant "Joe" in the rain.

75

Eugene Gloria is the author of four books of poems—*Sightseer in This Killing City* (Penguin Random House, 2019), winner of an Indiana Authors Award; *My Favorite Warlord* (Penguin, 2012), winner of the Anisfield-Wolf Book Award, *Hoodlum Birds* (Penguin, 2006), and *Drivers at the Short-Time Motel* (Penguin, 2000), a National Poetry Series selection and recipient of the Asian American Literary Award. His honors include a Fulbright Research Grant, a Pushcart Prize, a Poetry Society of America Award, and a Fulbright Senior Visiting Fellowship, among others. He has also received fellowships for residencies at MacDowell, Yaddo, Montalvo Arts Center, Djerassi Resident Artist Program, VCCA at Le Moulin à Nef (France), Fundación Valparaíso (Spain), Château de Lavigny (Switzerland), Nawat Fes (Morocco), Willapa Bay AiR, Virginia Center for the Creative Arts, and Ragdale Foundation. He is the chair of the English Department and a professor of Creative Writing at DePauw University.

Laurie Ann Guerrero

ON EATING RATTLESNAKE

03-14-2023

I remember it only once—I was small. Maybe it was
the one my father shot off the front porch, maybe it
wasn't. The men stood around the fire; the women sat
inside. I snaked around the men hiding myself:
slitherer. I have seen it many times, the long
stripping—one fist pulling skin, another pulling flesh.
And how the kills were celebrated: rattles and skins
hung like tapestries. The innards left to wild things.
When it was passed around, hot from the fire outside,
the women did not partake. I dug in, rough and
curious: there was nothing more unashamed than a
rattler. No apology in its tongue. It would never be
cute. I had to eat it. I had to know this.

Laurie Ann Guerrero, born and raised in the Southside of San Antonio, is the author of four collections: *Babies Under the Skin* (Panhandler 2008), *A Tongue in the Mouth of the Dying* (University of Notre Dame 2013), *A Crown for Gumecindo* (Aztlan Libre 2015), and *I Have Eaten the Rattlesnake: New & Selected* (TCU 2021). former Poet Laureate of the city of San Antonio (2014-2014) and the state of Texas (21016-2017), Guerrero holds a B.A. in English Language & Literature from Smith College and an MFA in poetry from Drew University. She is an Associate Professor and the Writer-in-Residence at Texas A&M University-San Antonio.

Tami Haaland

DEER ON CRAZY CREEK

10-07-2021

Along the trail I think how risky the venture,
the signs that say don't go alone into bear country.
I can see miles except in aspen. Walking uphill
in sage I think of Yellow Woman, of the stranger
who finds her and takes her into another life.
It's after that, after coming from a grove of trees,
I climb on a huge split boulder and watch
an ant navigate a forest of lichens. When I
raise my eyes to the horizon, I see you,
the way you hold your head, ambling
along the trail, the sway of your body on this
path made long before humans managed and
mapped this place. You are doing what we do:
head down, step ahead, step ahead.
When you look up and I begin to speak, you stop,
deciding whether to bolt or continue, a turn
for us both. I wonder, do your thoughts go to
the bear at the edge of the mind, the long trail
with golden butterflies on sage, flies that chase
and bite? Do you understand what calls
and calls again from an aspen horizon?

Lost Horse Press published Tami Haalands' fourth poetry collection, *If I Had Said Beauty*, in March 2025. Her poems have appeared in *Fugue, Cutthroat, The American Journal of Poetry, december, The Ecopoetry Anthology, Cascadia Field Guide*, and many other journals and anthologies. They have also been featured on *The Writer's Almanac, Verse Daily, American Life in Poetry*, and *The Slowdown*. Haaland is a former Montana Poet Laureate, a recipient of the Montana Governor's Humanities Award and Montana Artist Innovation Award.

Forrest Hamer

UNCLE

09-10-2018

My grandfather's brother was a gravedigger.

He was more than this, I am sure,

but he became little more than parable

to my mother who did not know him well,

who feared him. She says of him

that he was a soldier in the War,

and that he returned to Goldsboro different-

he kept to himself, paced the dirt streets at dusk,

and he begged for work in the graveyards.

After only three days of sculpting out graves,

his dusk time pacing became more agitated,

and he began then to talk back to the dead

still living alongside him. He shouted,

cursed at them, pleaded that they leave him alone

and that they return.

Forrest Hamer is the author of three collections of poems—*Call & Response* (1995, Alice James Books), *Middle Ear* (2000, Roundhouse Press), and *Rift* (2007, Four Way Books).

Sam Hamill

THE ORCHID FLOWER

10-02-2013

Just as I wonder
whether it's going to die,
the orchid blossoms

and I can't explain why it
moves my heart, why such pleasure

comes from one small bud
on a long spindly stem, one
blood red gold flower

opening at mid-summer,
tiny, perfect in its hour.

Even to a white-
haired craggy poet, it's
purely erotic,

pistil and stamen, pollen,
dew of the world, a spoonful

of earth, and water.
Erotic because there's death
at the heart of birth,

drama in those old sunrise
prisms in wet cedar boughs,

deepest mystery
in washing evening dishes
or teasing my wife,

who grows, yes, more beautiful
because one of us will die.

Hamill was the author of more than a dozen collections of poetry, including *Destination Zero: Poems 1970–1995, Almost Paradise: New and Selected Poems and Translations* (2005), *Measured by Stone* (2007), and *Habitation: Collected Poems* (2014). Influenced by Ezra Pound, William Carlos Williams, Kenneth Rexroth, Denise Levertov, and Hayden Carruth, Hamill "presents a model of honest, consistent, undisguised political engagement: he articulates not only a vision of peace with justice, not only his relish for work to achieve that vision, but his sense of the role that poetry can play," as *Publishers Weekly* noted in its review of *Measured by Stone*. Hamill has also published several collections of essays and numerous translations, including *Crossing the Yellow River: 300 Poems from the Chinese* (2000) and *Narrow Road to the Interior: And Other Writings* (2013). Hamill's own poetry has been translated into more than a dozen languages. Hamill was notably committed to moral issues. When First Lady Laura Bush invited him to a 2003 White House symposium on poetry, he declined in protest of the impending war in Iraq, and he instead launched poetsagainstthewar.org, an online anthology that has collected over 20,000 poems of protest and spawned an international movement. Hamill edited a collection of poems from the website, *Poets Against the War* (2003). Responding to critics who doubted the place of politics in poetry, Hamill noted in a 2006 interview, "You can't write about character and the human condition and be apolitical—that's not the kind of world we've ever lived in."

Jeff Hardin

FROM HERE TO THERE

08-10-07

My father wrestles with the chain, slams it
tangled toward the truckbed where it catches
tailgate, slither-clangs to a heap beneath
his feet. Like a serpent of heavy links.
Like the unwieldy weight his bogus life
has been, his trying to move it from here
to there. He curses God, who made him fail.
He turns, commands me pick up what I can.

I do: his stubborn will, his quiet code,
the all day bouts of walking through the yard
to find out what the moles have thieved. The stare.
The muscle pulled. The knife slammed down to hush
the dinner talk. I've heaved to get to here,
mid-life, his life, to pack it up for good.

Jeff Hardin is the author of seven books of poetry, most recently *Watermark, A Clearing Space in the Middle of Being,* and *No Other Kind of World.* His work has been honored with the Nicholas Roerich Prize, the Donald Justice Prize, and the X. J. Kennedy Prize. He lives and teaches in TN.

Gustavo Hernandez

WINTER CUMBIA WITH BROTHER AND SISTER

12-22-2020

for Elias and Adanari

Drinking in different cities, all three of us
end up in restaurants where the air is synthesized
lavender and a steady bass line anchoring a sedge
of crane calls mimicked by a keyboard.
With our red eyes perched
on neon, elbows on yellow plastic tabletops,
we watch the night break apart in drafts
and coats through automatic doors. Weeks
have passed since we last saw each other,
and maybe this soft splintering is what comes
after grief allows us some form
of breath. But out here on my own, I
can still see the ways in which we try
to remind and connect ourselves with memory.
Tonight it's by sharing the names of the songs
playing on the too-loud speakers bolted to the white
tile of these places, the times an accordion
unexpectedly completes a phrase and calls out
like a father in a sundown of reeds.

Gustavo Hernandez is the author of *bachelor* (flower song press, 2025) and *flower grand first* (moon tide press, 2021). He was born in jalisco, mexico and lives in southern california.

Lee Herrick

FLIGHT

2/11/2020

The in-flight magazine crossword partially done,
a corner begun here, scratched out answers there,
one set of answers in pencil, another in the green.
The woman with the green ball point knew
the all-time hit king is Rose and the Siem Reap
treasure is Angkor Wat. The woman, perhaps en route
to hold her dying mother's hand in Seattle, forgot
about death for ten minutes while remembering her
husband's Cincinnati Reds hat while gardening after
the diagnosis. Her handwriting was so clean. Maybe
she was a surgeon. Maybe a painter. No. What painter
wouldn't know 17 down, Diego's love, five letters?
In a rush, her dying mother's voice came back
to her, or maybe she was a Chinese adoptee and her mother's
imagined voice said, *wo ai ni*. At 30,000 feet,
you focus on 33 across, Asian American classic,
The Woman _____, when a stranger in the window
seat sees the clue, watches me write in W, and she says
Warrior, and for a moment you forget it is your favorite
memoir, and she reminds you of lilies or roses, Van Gogh
or stems with thorns, art galleries in romantic cities
where she is headed but you should not go. The flight
attendant grazes my shoulder. The crossword squares,
the letters, the chairs and aisles seem so tight in flight,
but there is nothing here but room, really.
Maybe the next passenger will know
what I do not: 64 down, five letters, Purpose.
And why do we remember what we do? We know
the buzz of Dickinson's fly and the number of years
in Marquez's solitude, but some things we will never
know, as it should be: why the body sometimes rumbles
like a plane hurtling over southern Oregon, how exactly
we fall in love, or if Frida and Maxine Hong
Kingston would have loved the same kind of tea.

Lee Herrick is the California Poet Laureate. He is the author of *In Praise of Late Wonder: New and Selected Poems* (Gunpowder Press, 2024) and three other books of poems, *Scar and Flower, Gardening Secrets of the Dead*, and *This Many Miles from Desire*. He co-edited *The World I Leave You: Asian American Poets on Faith and Spirit* and *Afterlives: An AGNI Portfolio of Asian Adoptee Diaspora Writing*. His writing appears widely in literary magazines, textbooks, and anthologies such as *Here: Poems for the Planet*, with an introduction by the Dalai Lama; *Indivisible: Poems of Social Justice*, with an introduction by Common; and *Dear America: Letters of Hope, Habitat, Defiance, and Democracy*, among others. Born in Daejeon, Korea and adopted to the United States at ten months, he served as Fresno Poet Laureate from 2015-2017. He is the 10th California Poet Laureate and the first Asian American to serve in the role.

Ishmael Angaluuk Hope

ARRANGEMENTS

08-24-2021

I will never stop looking at women–
creases, dimples, folds, hips swiveling,
scanning bookshelves, munching lasagna
and Caesar salad, sweat mingling
with lily petals and berry-soaked sod.

I look on in despair when a woman
with thick apple hips and a soft belly
wraps a sweater around her waist,
folding her back like a cat picked up
by the collar as she collects a magazine
from the coffee table. I want to tell her
there's nothing to be ashamed of, her body
is the cinnamon of life, sweet ambergris,
milk and honey. All trunk and root,
crow's feet, round face, locks of silver hair.
Chamber bells clang, Chinese silk drapes
over windows, flow blue serving
bowls piled with oranges. She walks
down the aisle over eight copper
shields. I steal rapid glances
other women notice anyway.

Ishmael Angaluuk Hope is a poet, game dev, Indigenous scholar, and actor who lives in Dzantik'ihéeni, Lingít Aaní. He published two books of poetry, *Courtesans of Flounder Hill* (Ishmael Reed Publications, 2014) *Rock Piles Along the Eddy* (Ishmael Reed Publications, 2017). His poetry has been published in several print and online publications and anthologies.

LeAnne Howe

MY NAME IS NOBLE SAVAGE

09-01-2021

I was built for iconography
Break my hymen
I bleed and reproduce
Children you sketch
 and photograph.
Catalogue,
But soon abandon.

How many wounds do you hope I carry?

My name is Noble Savage
Wanna rent me for a day?
A week?
A year?
By the hour?
I'm the story you finger-fucked
The evidence under your fingernail
Can you feel me coming for you?

My name is Noble Savage
You killed me
In other to bring me back to life
As your pet, a mascot
A man.
Since I'm your invention
Everything I say comes true.

My name is Noble Savage
America's redeemer.
Tonight,
alone with my murderer,
Iconographer
May your God have
Mercy on your soul.

Poet, fiction writer, filmmaker, and playwright LeAnne Howe was born and raised in Oklahoma and is a member of the Choctaw Nation of Oklahoma. She worked as a newspaper journalist for 12 years before earning an MFA from Vermont College. Howe's lyrical poems engage Native American life. She is the author of the poetry collection *Evidence of Red: Poems and Prose* (2005), which won the Oklahoma Book Award. Her novels include *Miko Kings: An Indian Baseball Story* (2007) and *Shell Shaker* (2001), which won the Before Columbus Foundation's American Book Award. The French translation of *Shell Shaker*, entitled *Equinoxes Rouge*, was a finalist for the 2004 Prix Médicis Etranger. Howe's scholarly articles have appeared in *Pre-removal Choctaw History: Exploring New Paths* (2008), *Reasoning Together: The Native Critics Collective* (2008), and *Foundations of First Peoples' Sovereignty: History, Culture, and Education* (2008). She was the narrator and host of the 2006 PBS documentary *Indian Country Diaries: Spiral of Fire*. Her plays include *The Mascot Opera: A Minuet*, which was commissioned by Minneapolis's Mixed Blood Theater in 2008. She performed her one-woman show *Choctalking on Other Realities* at the Krannert Center for the Performing Arts in 2009. She was an editor of the Norton anthology of Native American poetry *When the Light of the World Was Subdued, Our Songs Came Through* (2020).

TR Hummer

CORROSIVE LYRIC

10-28-2013

The fly that dissolves in the carnivorous pitcher
   of the bog plant; the bog, which breaks down
Tigers' bones but tans and supples their hides;
   the lump of ore wasted to sand by acid rain;
And the old man smoking at his corner desk
   who has burned himself alive with poetry.

About half a lifetime ago (mine, that is) I began to glimpse the possibility of a model of writing poems that it has taken me a long time to even begin to bring to real fruition. Perhaps I'm not there yet. Much of the model comes in fact from Whitman—a poet whom people often claim to emulate without even playing in the same concert hall. Whitman wrote out of the mind of the body politic. His "I" is not an "I" at all in the usual sense, even though it sometimes says "I am Walt Whitman." For him, this process was a celebratory hymn, though it darkens over time, especially after the Civil War. We live on in that darkness Whitman began to discern on his horizon, but the need of the citizen in his or her tiny body to speak to, and out of, and for, and against, the big body that is the aggregate of the nation, or of the human race itself, is still with us. I speak as a single cell, or maybe one chromosome in the DNA of humanity, but I do so with the conviction that, done right, such speaking matters to the body of the whole. Metaphorically, I try to help inject dopamine into the synapses of humankind.

Poet, critic, and editor T.R. Hummer was born in 1950 in Macon, Mississippi. He holds degrees from the University of Southern Mississippi and the University of Utah, where he earned a PhD. Though his early work is reminiscent of Southern writers such as James Dickey, Hummer's poetry considers a range of experiences and ideas. His interest in class, sexuality, music, and metaphysics shape collections such as *Lower-Class Heresy* (1987), *The Eighteen-Thousand-Ton Olympic Dream* (1990), *Walt Whitman in Hell* (1996), *The Infinity Sessions* (2005), and *Ephemeron* (2011).

Major Jackson

LEAVING SATURN
—SUN RA & HIS YEAR 2000 MYTH SCIENCE ARKESTRA
AT GRENDEL'S LAIR CABARET, 1986

05-02-10

Skyrocketed—
My eyes dilate old
Copper pennies.
Effortlessly, I play
*

Manifesto of the One
Stringed Harp. Only
This time I'm washed
Ashore, ship-wrecked
*

In Birmingham.
My black porcelain
Fingers, my sole
Possession. So I
*

Hammer out
Equations for
A New Thing.
Ogommetelli,
*

Ovid & Homer
Behind me, I toss
Apple peelings in
The air & half-hear
*

Brush strokes, the up
Kick of autumn
Leaves, the Arkestra
Laying down for
*

New dimensions.
I could be at Berkeley

Teaching a course—
Fixin's: How to Dress
*

Myth or Generations:
Spaceships in Harlem.
Instead, vibes from Chi-
Town, must be Fletcher's
*

Big Band Music—oh,
My brother, the wind—
& know this life is
Only a circus. I'm
*

Brushed aside: a naif,
A charlatan, too avant
Garde. Satellite music for
A futuristic tent, says
*

One critic. Heartbreak
In outer space, says
Another,— lunar
Dust on the brain.
*

I head to NewYork.
NewYork loves
A spectacle: wet pain
Of cement, sweet
*

Scent of gulls swirling
Between skyscrapers
So tall, looks like war.
If what I'm told is true

90

*

Mars is dying, it's after
The end of the world.
So, here I am,
In Philadelphia,
*

Death's headquarters,
Here to save the cosmos,
Here to dance in a bed
Of living gravestones.

When I was younger, I became obsessed with Sun Ra. I collected his albums which were rare productions in themselves. From the album cover to the final product, all was independently produced. But more I was enthralled with Sun Ra's understanding of the role of his music which was to save the earth. This notion of saving mankind, as well as his pun on Noah's Ark and Orchestra, (he was full of witticisms, that added up to serious equations for our discovery) is utterly familiar to those of us who grew up in the church, but more it resonated with a spiritual and communal purpose I had begun to understand and attribute to artists of all genres and disciplines, least of all, my own writings at that time.

Major Jackson is the author of *Razzle Dazzle: New and Selected Poems*. He teach teaches at Vanderbilt University.

Jessica Jacobs

PRIMER

10-02-2019

A Florida child knows the safest part
of a lake is the middle. That gators
and moccasins shade in the lilies, hunker
shoreline in the muck just past
the trucked-in sand. Knows a snake egg
means a mother's nearby, and angry.
That to kill her, you must bring a shovel
down right behind her skull—leave
too much neck and the headed half will keep
coming at you. Knows to run zigzag if a gator
gives chase, their squat digger legs built
for speed, not for turning. Has a friend
who has a friend who lost a thumb
to a snapping turtle, has worn live lizards
as earrings, watched lake-caught minnows
devour a store-bought birthday
goldfish. Has been dragged on a field trip
to a sinkhole wide as a roller rink:
a red truck at the bottom, wheels up;
along with half a house and a wreck
of toys and books. Has been told it happened
on a day like any other. Has gone home
to tread water at the lake's calming
center; cool streamers of springs fluttering
her thighs, the sun a constant; the sucking
sound of a bathplug pulled, her imagination.

Jessica Jacobs is the author of *unalone, poems in conversation with the Book of Genesis* (four Way Books, 2024); *Take Me with You, Wherever You're Going* (four Way Books, 2019), one of *Library Journal's* Best Poetry Books of the Year, winner of the Devil's Kitchen and Goldie Awards, and a finalist for the Brockman-Campbell, American fiction, and Julie Suk Book Awards; and *Pelvis with Distance* (White Pine Press, 2015), a biography-in-poems of Georgia O'Keeffe, winner of the New Mexico Book Award in Poetry and a finalist for the Lambda Literary Award; and the co-author of *Write It! 100 Poetry Prompts to Inspire* (Spruce Books/Penguin RandomHouse). She is the founder and executive director of Yetzirah: A Hearth for Jewish Poetry.

Luke Johnson

BEE FENNEL

08-21-2019

I trapped bees in boxes
& carried them to the neighbor's blind son.

Set them loose. Praised their frantic undulations,
their search for someone to serve,

then left him, bitten, tongue partly swollen,
stomach distended & scabbed. Edit: I did not

simply set them free in the blind boy's hair. I
wooed them with candy & blew smoke through

a hole in the box until they dropped dizzy.
Plucked their stingers. Drowned the queen

& smiled as her wings folded into soda pop.
Promised the boy a taste of fennel, hot joy

thrumming his throat. He opened. Teeth
clean. Teeth like washed windows. Tasted

my kiss. Unraveled my tongue inside his.

Luke Johnson is the author of *Quiver* (Texas Review Press), a finalist for the Jake Adam York Award, The Vassar Miller Prize, and The Levis Award; *A Slow Indwelling* (Harbor Editions); and *Distributary* (Texas Review Press). *Quiver* was named one of four finalists for the 2024 California Book Award. Johnson was selected by Patricia Smith as a finalist for the esteemed 2024 Robert frost Residency through Dartmouth College. You can find more of his work at *Kenyon Review*, *Prairie Schooner*, *Narrative Magazine*, *Poetry Northwest* and elsewhere.

Judy Jordan

AFTER THE FARMER'S MARKET

11-24-2015

In this hoofed hour before dawn,
          in the flustered scuttle of small animals

in underbrush and leaf flutter intent in their clawed search. Shot

moon and scumbled cloud, screech owl and bobcat scream. Moth,

bat, and souls of the newly dead flitting leaf to leaf.

In the smell of honeysuckle and angel heart,

in the tick of each star clicking off
and darkness drifting
toward its concession to day's factory of heat and glare,

wake, wake, rise and go
through these empty streets to meet that sunrise of
smelted coins hot with the grief of many hands.

Wake, wake, wake,
          get up, get up, and go now.

In this hour of terror,
          birds crying out,

crying to the blood, to the bitter reek, to
the spilled guts of the night's hunted,

scattered chirps and screeches sifting in wind,
rustling through tree limbs, easing down like a preened feather
to settle in the nests of woven grasses and weeds.

In this hour of the dead,
          get up, get up, and go.

Prowl the steaming, empty streets. Follow the bristle-brushed
truck along the dreary wave of asphalt as the grumbling,
diesel-belching beast hoses yesterday into the gutters.

Get up and go past the rail yard and feed stores,
past the vestibules and crumbling doorways of hunger and no sleep,
past the drunks swaying on the curb's edge,
cabbies getting high in their cars as they wait out the hours,
                              the horrible and lonely hours.

Now, in the crooked teeth of dawn,
in the growl and lolling tongue,
                        everything else must wait.

The runaways who scour parking lots,
                     heel-to-toe,
for any dropped thing,

ghosts of the black-owned businesses, barbershops
and doctor's offices bulldozed to build this pedestrian mall,

ghosts who hover here with the blue fog,
ghosts squeezed fish-eyed under the ridged mountains,
ghosts slipping along this street with its lobbed and slab-
sided board and batten and drywall houses, must wait.
                                         Ghosts

who climb up the slink and squeak
of the narrow steps to the one-room,
fourth floor walk-up where Ming-Loy shares a cot
with her five-year-old daughter who must wait,
             wait for the tea kettle to scream out,

wait for Ming-Loy to pour this long lick of sinewy water over her
crouched in a tin bucket, wait for her to say, Broken plumbing.
Cheap rent,
          wait for the leftovers I will take her,

vegetables, cut flowers, it all, it all, it all must wait now
for I must get up, get up, rise and go.

Home at three AM
from the pizza delivery job, up at five with the shrieking birds. Get up and go.

Oh do not think
of how little will be made, six hours in the heat-scorched lot,
bone-honed blade of exhaustion

edging up the ladder of my back
with my small offerings of coneflowers,
tomatoes and yellow squash
curled in on themselves like question marks,
for the sweating hoards of dimes and nickels,
damp wrinkle of dollar bills,
just get up, get up, pack the truck and go.

◊

The letter, picked up off the street said,
so I've found you. What you're doing is time. Jail time
is the longest time. When I see you again it won't be in there
but out here. Here's a twenty for you. Say goodbye
to Toto. We're not in Kansas anymore.

◊

The gout-legged man resting on the bench said,
You have to keep one leg out of your pants
when you take a crap. So you don't get trapped.
That's what you have to do in jail.

◊

The man shouted into his cell phone, That's what I get
for trusting damned, no-good, lazy, white trash.

◊

And Luna, who sold incense and hand-made soap, is dead.

And Regina, the muffin-queen, who waited a year

so Blue Cross would cover her back's busted disc,
ignoring blood in her stools, cancer's filed teeth
gnawing along her colon, is dead.

◊

I have seen the women piling from their pimps' Caddies,
seen them spread through the streets
like a rare virus seeping organ to organ,
have seen the sheriff's notice nailed on the door, RENT PAST DUE,

family photos, marksman medals, all the trivia of years
and lives the landlord hauls to the dumpster, ground up
by the trash truck as if in Polyphemus' gaping jaws,
have seen the heavy-booted men splattered with concrete,

hunched at the bar, dull-eyed through the sitcom's canned laughter,
their entire lives laid out before them like a rough-stitched corpse
trundled into its cold slot after the coroner's knife,
and I, no Lazarus, sores licked by dogs, not wrenched

from Abraham's arms, not risen from the dead to warn
the rich man's brothers, only a piping voice that begs the stars
to cast their cold, lidless gaze onto me as I plead that I not die
in such a wrong time, such a wrong place.

◊

Now the sun directly overhead so I must
reload the unsold coreopsis, drooping columbine,
               vegetables, sun-bruised and soft,
even as they come,
                  those who know the closing hours,
who know the cull of bruised peaches and over-grown squash.

They spill from their rust-shot four-doors,
cars held together with tar, duct tape,
                              clothes hangers and string.
Washed in this warped and ruined light,
                  a dime store daubing, a bad draft,
I wait here and want to know what happened

to that life I signed up for,
the one with chubby cheeks and blonde hair,
            the freckle-spattered nose and easy smile.

I wait and watch as they wave away yellow jackets
from the mesh-metal trash cans, watch
string-haired teenagers turn their backs on mothers
who pull out worm-gnawed eggplant and yellowing cucumbers.

            Oh how fragile, how frail
this thing we call a body: How desperate and tender
it all seems: Those scant few years ago
when I stood outside any fast food joint,
            too skinny, gulping the grease stink,

and just last year, lugging boulders, splitting wood, then, the burst disc,
            pain tunneling down my hamstring,

and now these sullen teenagers, pacing
this parking lot, pretending not to know
their own mothers whose arms are swallowed
by trash cans, who scratch their nails against the melon's mushy rind
and I hold out the blood--red tomatoes, the milky corn:

            Come, I whisper,
come, I cry out like some ancient song, a song of hunger,
                        a song of sorrow,
and they creep from the trash cans, the wrecked cars, the blind alleys,
creep from all the hiding places of the poor,
as hunger, musk--mouthed hunger, lumbers from its dark doorway.

**A long poem is a covenant. You're asking the reader to walk with
you longer than they normally would—through fire, through fog,
through flood. For their time, you must offer gifts. Not just once,
not just at the end, but every few lines. Rhythm. Image. Music.
Simile so charged it rewires the body. These are the offerings that
keep a reader with you. The long poem must move with necessity.**

It cannot simply repeat what it knows. It must deepen, widen, fracture, transform. You can use motif as spine—sound, symbol, line—but what returns must return changed. A root must split stone. A line must throb differently after the page turns. It must have momentum that gathers heat and burns. That momentum must carry the reader through the flood, the fire, off the cliff's edge.

Judy Jordan's first book of poetry, Carolina Ghost Woods, won the 1999 Walt Whitman Award from the Academy of American Poets, the 2000 National Book Critics Circle Award, as well as the Utah Book of the Year Award, the OAY Award from the Poetry Council of North Carolina, and the Thomas Wolfe Literary Award. Her second book of poetry, Sixty Cent Coffee and a Quarter to Dance, was published by LSU press. Her third book, Hunger, was published by Tinderbox Editions. Her fourth book Children of Salt is forthcoming from Tinderbox. She has recently completed a novel, Broken Days, Broken Hearts and is currently working on a memoir, My Mama, My Sweet Nelly. Jordan built her own environmentally friendly earthbag and cob house off-grid surrounded by the Shawnee National Forest, and teaches creative writing at Southern Illinois University, Carbondale. mics.siu.edu/humanities-social-sciences/english/faculty/jordan-judy.php

Allison Joseph

THE WORLD'S WORST JUKEBOX

09-07-2017

plays every song you've ever hated—
maudlin country ballads and stupid novelty hits,
syrupy pop ditties from the Seventies—
tunes so chipper and insistent
you still know them after twenty years,
can remember how these songs sounded
coming out of your hand-held radio,
hiss slithering from the cheap transistor,
static marking spaces between stations.
It's hard to fathom why
someone would put tunes this bad together,
deliberate cruelty, you think,
as you lean over the shimmering machine
in search of one good song
for your shiny quarter.
You can't deal with hearing
the Captain and Tennille gush
that love will keep them together,
but your other choices are no better—
the Swedish schmaltz of Abba's "Dancing Queen,"
the disco version of the theme from Star Wars,
Chuck Berry's number one embarrassment,
"My Ding-A-Ling." There's no Beatles or Stones
on this Wurlitzer, just bland British Invasion wimps
Chad and Jeremy, that foolish chronicle
of the c.b. craze, Convoy, the simpering corn
of David Gates and Bread. No Sly Stone or Prince
and the Revolution either, but "Kung Fu Fighting"
instead, a song whose phony martial arts shouts
thrilled us all when were eight.
Groups no one's heard of since
their one chart hit live on in infamy
here: the breathy vocals of Andrea True,
former porn star, the disembodied female chants

100

of Silver Convention, another Eurodisco product
of interchangeable singers. There are
two different versions of "Muskrat Love,"
every smarmy hit by Air Supply,
and singles from bands whose very names
are bad omens: Vanilla Fudge, the Chipmunks,
Pink Lady. You want to grab someone, anyone,
to collar the bar's manager
for an explanation, demanding the name
of who did this, threatening to storm his house
to ask how anyone could give us a jukebox
with no Supremes or Vandellas, but
with the Crystals singing
"He Hit Me And It Felt Like A Kiss,"
a dirge with lyrics so vile
few stations ever played it,
a song no one will punch,
not even on this jukebox.

Allison Joseph lives in Carbondale, Illinois, where she is a professor of English and
director of the MFA Program in Creative Writing at Southern Illinois University.
She serves as poetry editor of *Crab Orchard Review*. Her books include *My
Father's Kites* (Steel Toe Books), *Trace Particles* (Backbone Press), *Little Epiphanies*
(NightBallet Press), *Mercurial* (Mayapple Press), *Mortal Rewards* (White Violet
Press), *Multitudes* (Word Poetry), *The Purpose of Hands* (Glass Lyre Press), *Double
Identity* (Singing Bone Press), *Corporal Muse* (Sibling Rivalry Press), and *What Once
You Loved* (Barefoot Muse Press). Her most recent full-length collection, *Confessions
of a Barefaced Woman*, was published by Red Hen Press in June 2018.

Brigit Pegeen Kelly

THE DRAGON

10-12-08

The bees came out of the junipers, two small swarms
The size of melons; and golden, too like melons,
They hung next to each other, at the height of a deer's breast
Above the wet black compost. And because
The light was very bright it was hard to see them,
And harder still to see what hung between them.
A snake hung between them. The bees held up a snake,
Lifting each side of his narrow neck, just below
The pointed head, and in this way, very slowly
They carried the snake through the garden,
The snake's long body hanging down, its tail dragging
The ground, as if the creature were a criminal
Being escorted to execution or a child king
To the throne. I kept thinking the snake
Might be a hose, held by two ghostly hands,
But the snake was a snake, his body green as the grass
His tail divided, his skin oiled, the way the male member
Is oiled by the female's juices, the greenness overbright,
The bees gold, the winged serpent moving silently
Through the air. There was something deadly in it,
Or already dead. Something beyond the report
Of beauty. I laid my face against my arm, and there
It stayed for the length of time it takes two swarms
Of bees to carry a snake through a wide garden,
Past a sleeping swan, past the dead roses nailed
To the wall, past the small pond. And when
I looked up the bees and the snake were gone,
But the garden smelled of broken fruit, and across
the grass a shadow lay for which there was no source,
A narrow plinth dividing the garden, and the air
Was like the air after a fire, or before a storm,
Ungodly still, but full of shapes turning.

Kelly's first collection of poems, *To The Place of Trumpets* (Yale University Press, 1987), was selected by James Merrill for the Yale Series of Younger Poets. *Song* (BOA Editions), which followed in 1995, was the 1994 Lamont Poetry Selection of the Academy of American Poets. Her third collection, *The Orchard* (BOA Editions, 2004), was a finalist for the Pulitzer Prize in Poetry, the Los Angeles Times Book Award in Poetry, and the National Book Critics Circle Award in Poetry. Her work has also appeared in several volumes of the Pushcart Prize Anthology and several volumes of *The Best American Poetry*.

Suji Kwock Kim

GENERATION

11-09-2011

0

Once I was nothing: once we were one.

1

In the unborn world we heard the years hurtling past,

whirring like gears in a giant factory—*time time time*—

2

We heard human breathing,

thoughts coming and going like bamboo leaves hissing in wind,

doubts swarming like reconnaissance planes over forests of sleep,

we heard words murmured in love.

3

We felt naked bodies climb each other,

cleaving, cleaving,

as if they could ride each other to a country that can't be named.

We felt bedsprings creak, felt the rough sailcloth of sheets dampen,

felt wet skin hold them together and apart.

What borders did they cross? What more did they want?

Bittersweet the sweat we tasted, the swollen lips we touched, the chafe of separate loins:

bittersweet the wine of *one flesh* they drank and drank.

4

They called us over oceans of dream-salt,

their voices *moving over the face of the waters* like searchlights from a guardtower.

We hid, and refused to come out.

Their cries followed like police dogs snarling from a leash.

We ran through benzene rain, flew through clouds of jet-fuel.

We swam through hydrogen spume, scudded among stars numberless as sands.

We didn't want to be born we didn't want.

Blindly their hands groped for us like dragnets trawling for corpses,

blindly their hands hauled me like grappling hooks from the waves,

the foaming scalps of ghost-children laughing, seeweed-hair dripping,

the driftwood of other children who might have been.

Out of chromosomes and dust,

cells of hope, cells of history,

out of refugees running from mortar shells, immigrants driving to power plants in Jersey,

out of meadowsweet and oil, the chaff of unlived lives blowing endlessly,

out of wishes known and unknown they reeled me in.

5

I entered the labyrinth of mother's body.

I wandered through nerve-forests branching in every direction,

towering trees fired by feeling, crackling and smoldering.

I rowed though vein-rivers.

I splashed in lymph-creeks between islands of glands.

I leaped rib to rib, rung to rung on the spine,

I swung from the ropes of entrails.

I clambered over tectonic plates of the skull, scrambling not to fall

down the chasms between, the mind-mountains where I could see no bottom.

I peered through sockets at the brain brewing in cliffs of bone

like a gigantic volcano, with its magma of memories, magma of tomorrows.

I could have played there forever, watching, wondering at the vast expanses inside,

wondering at the great chambers in the heart.

What machine made me move into the womb-cave, made me

a grave of flesh, now the engine of beginning driving forwards,

cells dividing, cells dividing:

now neurons sizzling, dendrites buzzing,

now arteries tunneling tissue like tubes hooked to an IV;

now organs pumping, hammers of hunger and thirst pounding,

now sinews cleaving, tendons lashing meat to bone:

meanwhile my skeleton welding, scalp cementing like mortar,

meanwhile my face soldered on, hardening like a mask of molten steel,

meanwhile my blood churning like a furnace of wanting,

meanwhile my heart ticking like a bomb—*is-was, is-was:*

then cold metal tongs clamped my forehad and temples,

then forceps plucked me from mother's body like fruit torn from a tree:

then I heard a cry of pain—mine? not mine?—

then a scalpel's *snip snip* against the umbilical cord, like razors scraping a leather strop:

soon I felt sticky with blood and matted fur, surgical lights blinding,

soon I felt tears burning my skin—*Why are you crying? Why am I?*—

I didn't know who or what I was, only that I was,

each question answered by the echo of my voice alone: I, I, I.

Suji Kwock Kim is the author of Notes from the Divided Country, which received the Walt Whitman Award from the Academy of American Poets (selected by Yusef Komunyakaa), the Addison Metcalf Award from the American Academy of Arts and Letters (selected by Charles Simic), the Whiting Writers' Award, the Bay Area Book Reviewers/Northern California Book Award, The Nation/"Discovery" Award, and was a finalist for the Griffin Prize. Her other works include Private Property, a multimedia play performed at the Edinburgh Festival Fringe; Notes from the North, which received the UK's International Book & Pamphlet Award (selected by Michael Schmidt, Neil Astley, Amy Wack); and Disorient: Fugues & Assimilamentations (forthcoming, W.W. Norton, U.S. and Canada; Chatto & Windus/ Penguin Random House UK, Ireland, and Commonwealth). She's currently a Hodder Fellow at Princeton University, a UNESCO-Bucheon Writer-in-Residence, a Royal Society of Literature Scriptorium Writer-in-Residence, and serves as a Trustee for the UK Charity Commission and CNK, formerly the European Alliance for Human Rights in North Korea, based in New Malden, Surrey, home to the largest community of North Korean refugees in the world outside Asia.

James Kimbrell

MT. PISGAH

01-19-2007

It was the middle of the night and I had lived
A long time with that country, with the hay
Rakes and rock paths and the beam bridge
Above the snake-thick waters. It was
The middle of the night so far into the field
The deer began not to notice the moons
In the shallow bean row puddles. That's how dark
Fell over the road that led into town and kept us
All from moving. Still, when the train passed,
Milk shook in its bucket and the earth sank
In a little. So each year when the corn shrank
Back to stubble, the mud strewn with husks,
More than anything silence grew tall there
Between the kitchen window and the shed's
Roof and the one note rust made in the stuck
Weather vane, in the rooster holding north.

James Kimbrell was born in Jackson, Mississippi in 1967. He has published three volumes of poetry: *Smote* (2015), *My Psychic* (2006), and *The Gatehouse Heaven* (1998), and was co-translator of *Three Poets of Modern Korea: Yi Sang, Hahm Dong-Seon, and Choi Young-Mi* (2002), all with Sarabande Books. His work has appeared in magazines such as *Poetry, Ploughshares, Field,* and *Best American Poetry, 2012.* He has been the recipient of the Discovery / The Nation Award, a Whiting Writer's Award, the Ruth Lilly Fellowship, the Bess Hokin Prize from *Poetry* magazine, and a fellowship from the National Endowment for the Arts. He lives in Tallahassee where he is a professor in the creative writing program at Florida State University.

Christine Kitano

SKY COUNTRY

09-14-2017

The Korean word for heaven is *ha-neul nara*, a kenning that translates literally to "sky country." It was a word often used by potential immigrants to describe the United States.

1.

My grandmother hoards gold dollar-coins, the heavy discs etched with Sacagawea's over-the-shoulder glance, an infant son tied in a blanket to her back. She doesn't know who Sacagawea is, or Lewis and Clark, or figures from most stories we read in elementary school. Instead, the Bible and Hollywood sculpt her history. Over dinner she'll re-enact the events in The Ten Commandments: she raises her arms, as if in victory, to summon the Pillar of Fire and split the Red Sea, her small hands pushing apart two walls of water so that Charlton Heston can arrive safely on the bank. "Yes," she'll nod, soup dripping from her chin. "That's exactly how it happened."

2.

My Korean is weak. I understand only pieces of what she says. But from her cycle of stories, familiar nouns and images emerge. 1953: Pregnant with my mother, my grandmother flees south, my aunt strapped to her back. (At this point, my aunt will point to her bowed legs, the calves that curve outward below the knees, as evidence of this journey.) There is always a boat, a river, and a fire. My grandmother runs toward one and away from another but someone, perhaps my grandfather, grabs her hand to pull her back. I don't know why. There are men, Korean men and American men. She tells them her name, or that she's pregnant, but I never understand how or if they respond. Often, the stories end with her turning around to find her husband has vanished.

3.

Heaven. Sky Country. In America, the streets overflow with milk and honey.

For stealing day-old donuts, my mother is fired from her first American job, cleaning offices in a downtown Los Angeles high-rise.

Still, this is America. America is good, she says. You don't know how good you have it here.

4.

I return to Los Angeles for New Year's. My grandmother asks where I live now and tries to pronounce the words: New York. Is it hot or cold there, she asks. Is there Korean food? Is there a church? She asks if New York is where President Bush lives, then what will happen if America loses the war. Would I raise the Iraqi flag, give up English for Arabic? I want to tell her it's not that kind of war, but I don't have the words. She cackles. "You don't know," she says.

5.

My grandmother speaks Korean but, a child of colonial Korea, reads and writes in Japanese. Now, of course, she conducts her life in English. She worries what I'll do with an English degree, not because of the "adjunct situation" or the overall decline of the humanities, but because she knows countries are not the concrete, black-outlined shapes that seem so permanent when we open our textbooks. She knows how history can wipe away a person's language. She's been the real civilian I can only try to imagine when I read articles in the newspaper over hot coffee.

It's my grandmother who ran, four months pregnant, five-year-old daughter clasped to her back. It's she who pleaded and begged, who prayed that a soldier would listen when she screamed her name. It's her home that was severed by an arbitrary line, her family, like a brittle branch, snapped down the middle.

6.

After the traditional dinner of dumpling soup, my grandmother calls me over, unzips the small pocket on her backpack. She takes out a wrinkled manila envelope. Inside are one hundred gold dollar-coins. She's been collecting all year, trading for them at the Mexican grocery and the Hollywood Park racetrack. I thank her, but tell her not to go through all the trouble, that they aren't worth more than paper money. She shrugs. "You don't know," she says.

Christine Kitano is the author of two collections of poetry, *Sky Country* (BOA Editions, 2017), and *Birds of Paradise* (Lynx House Press, 2011). *Sky Country* won the Central New York Book Award and was a finalist for the Paterson Poetry Prize. Her chapbook, *Dumb Luck & other poems* (Texas Review Press, 2024) won the Robert Phillips Chapbook Prize. She co-edited the oral history collection *Who You? Hawai'i Issei* (University of Hawai'i / Japanese Cultural Center of Hawai'i Press, 2017) and *They Rise Like a Wave: An Anthology of Asian American Women's Poetry* (Blue Oak Press, 2022). She is an associate professor at Stony Brook University where she teaches in the MFA and BFA programs in Creative Writing and Literature. She has served on the faculty for the MFA Program for Writers at Warren Wilson College since 2018.

Ruth Ellen Kocher

COSMOGONY

09-29-2025

i begin with ocean
floating in the free space of my ribs
somewhere between
ursa major and ursa minor
i begin in scorpio
a car ride into the city
before andromeda collided with the milky way another timeline ago
i begin as a cluster of muscadine grapes bursting bloody on their stems
i begin at the end
hungry
gorged on the ill-shaped stars which had
not yet begun
i begin beaten by my own hands
a comet galaxy
orbiting the parking lot of stumblin' inn friday nights waiting for a wrong
turn
in the right car
i begin as a side bet
a detour into cosmos
via the elliptical path of my thumbprint
i begin as magellan's cloud hovering above
a cartwheel galaxy before magellan imagined himself
i begin as a call into
the deep-deep
as a black eye begging my way into medusa merger
i begin
as something found and then lost
as a clutch meaning a small group
as in a small group of mothers huddled around a baby fever-charged

i begin with nothing

no history no moons

I imagine nothing and
nothing begins

Ruth Ellen Kocher is the author of the poetry collections *Third Voice* (Tupelo Press, 2016), *domina Un/blued* (Tupelo Press 2013), *Ending in Planes* (Noemi Press, 2013), *One Girl Babylon* (New Issues Press 2003), *When the Moon Knows You're Wandering*, winner of the Green Rose Prize in Poetry (New Issues Press 2002), and *Desdemona's Fire*, winner of the Naomi Long Madget Award for African American Poets (Lotus Press 1999). Her poems have been translated into Persian in the Iranian literary magazine, She'r, and have appeared or are forthcoming in various anthologies including, Angles of Ascent: A Norton Anthology of Contemporary African American Poets, Black Nature, From the Fishouse: An Anthology of Poems that Sing, Rhyme, Resound, Syncopate, Alliterate, and Just Plain Sound Great, An Anthology for Creative Writers: The Garden of ForkingPaths, IOU: New Writing On Money, New Bones: Contemporary Black Writing in America. She has taught poetry writing for the University of Missouri, Southern Illinois University, the New England College Low Residency MFA program, the Indiana Summer Writer's workshop, and Washington University's Summer Writing program.

Jason Koo

BEGIN, BEING, BEGIN

02-03-2024

We are too late for the gods, and too early
for Being. Reading Heidegger again. Tried

Tolstoy's *What Is Art?* but he started
delving into the history of Christian art

and it is way too early in the day and late
in civilization to be lectured on the history

of Christian art. All those museums filled
with mute, flat paintings I dutifully tried

to show interest in, though I was bored to death,
or worse, next-to-death, death-in-life.

Being's poem, just begun, is man. To think
is to confine yourself to a single thought

that one day stands still like a star
in the world's sky. A single thought

is hard. Already Heidegger's had at least
three of those whereas I have had none

except his. The beautiful distillation of the brain,
only received in the early light of morning

when distractions and anxieties have not yet
haunted you down. In thinking all things

become solitary and slow. Patience nurtures
magnanimity. You can feel his patience

and magnanimity in just those three words,
slowly wheeled into place like great stones.

He who thinks greatly must err greatly.
I put a star next to that passage, perhaps

because of what I believe it allows
me. Yes, that awkward little enjambment

was deliberate. The little me, squiggled out
of the line, morsel of the me-al dropped

for the dogs. Concession after concession
one allows oneself as the real thinking me

gets deferred, the begin in Being never
begins. How often, in trying to type *begin*,

I've typed *being*, as if my unconscious
were reminding me of something still unborn.

But never do I seem to mistype *begin*
for *being*. The artist is the origin of the work.

The work is the origin of the artist.
Anyone can easily see that we are moving

in a circle. When I like a book, as I like
this one, I paw at the pages, claw my fingers

through the stack, put my face against
their thingly character. The work as work

sets up a world. The work holds open
the Open of the world. I love this so much

I can't even tell you, though obviously
I just told you, though the more obviously

probably the less I told you. What is spoken
is never, and in no language, what is said.

I am thinking of putting these quotes
on a page for my poetry students, so they can

begin to understand what the work is.
But probably they will stare and fidget.

I have never asked this question in workshop
and maybe I should: Is this a *work*?

Does it open up a world? Does it hold open
the Open of the world? Some questions,

I think, to silence the presumptions always
brewing. When I look at a student poem,

I'm not even thinking of these questions
at first, because that would be unbearable.

Once an MAT student asked me to make
a rubric for how I graded poems, thinking

this would improve her grade. I said,
Believe me, you do not want to see this rubric.

But I spent so much time on this poem, I
worked so hard on it, my grade never improves

or only a little, I have no idea what you want.
Well, how much time did you spend on it?

A couple hours. First part of my rubric
would be You must spend at least four or five

consecutive hours on the poem, must sit there
until you have no idea what you are doing

becomes what you are doing, must sit there
until the blank of being makes a beginning.

Make sense? Thought so. So maybe I'll just take
a point and a half off for all your tense shifts?

Jason Koo is a second-generation Korean American poet. He is the author of four full-length collections of poetry, including, most recently, *No Rest*, winner of the Eugene Paul Nassar Poetry Prize and the Diode Editions Book Contest and a finalist for AWP's Donald Hall Prize for Poetry; and *More Than Mere Light*, *America's Favorite Poem* and *Man on Extremely Small Island*. His work has been published in the *American Scholar*, *Best American Poetry*, *Missouri Review*, *Village Voice* and *Yale Review*, among other places, and won fellowships from the National Endowment for the Arts, Vermont Studio Center and New York State Writers Institute. He is an associate teaching professor of English and the director of creative writing at Quinnipiac University and the founder of Brooklyn Poets. He lives in Beacon, New York.

Ed Bok Lee

MITOCHONDRIAL EVENING

03-20-2025

One tiny piece of our DNA is inherited only down the female line....
Some molecular biologists say that, aeons ago, the mitochondrion
was a free-living organism with its own DNA....
—"Mitochondrial DNA: The Eve Gene,"
by Stephen Oppenheimer

There is a woman and a man
naked inside me, though
they have yet to properly meet.
This started long ago, before
time; before memory
or art; when ocean caves
were umbilical. The woman
and man morphed over millennia,
trading notochords and ectoderms,
but this remained constant: he loved
when the woman sang in joy,
in sadness; he loved
that he, the man, could never
enter into her voice without
leaving behind all he knew how to savage
for their children. Eventually,
he fashioned a tail to better
find her, and she more sensitive
filaments and corona. His
greatest gift, the shoulder
he built to hurl slings. Soon,
together, they willed the best vista
from the height of a mountain.
Grottos filled with skulls.
Meanwhile, he honed consonants;
she polished her vowels. Time
hammered bronze to shield
safety from chaos. Still their children

escaped through the days and years.
Still the woman and man, mid-winter,
traded turns stomping off
into darkness. Fierce
declarations. She within the man inside her
daughters and sons could only
listen to him paint
disturbing glyphs of his mother's
dreams. This man, you see, despite
sharpened tools, did not yet understand
no document is imperishable;
any immutable covenant
has no name. The woman
suffocating in her own father's nightmares
invented faith. The man drowning
in his mother's grief cursed anyone fearful.
Their children stoked the fire. Sometimes
I hear them, my man and woman,
arguing, or making love,
it's not always clear. One
person inside me, my great
-great-grandmother, whispers
to her lover on a straw mat
that one day they will escape
to a beautiful country where
people can marry whomever they wish.
The one atop the other smiles, wonders
what it would be like far beyond
this family's rice fields. Giggling
in the cellar of a pavilion, breaths
like fragrant soup, they kiss
then oversleep.
                    Far away, a distant
ancestor within my great-grandfather
is at war, fleeing barbarians,
communists, giant hyenas, drones.
Every decision he makes will determine
eight percent of the planet's chromosomes.
One daughter inside him will love the lute
so well my ears slightly protrude.
In a world ruled by women, the saying goes,

there would be no war. At least one
mean girl inside me is skeptical.
The old man selling arrows, seeds, and
parchment in my spine only really wants to skip
stones across water. Everyone within his daughter's
wavy hair murmurs: it all depends
on the quality of love inherited
through one's parents.
                        Where
did any mother end and a father begin
if all marriages not a century back
came with keys to her ovaries? For eons
the women inside me have taught
their most prideful brothers how to let go.
For eons the men inside me have
fought to burn and rebuild. To where,
in which direction? asks
one to the other, now lost in a forest
fairy tale that slithers like syntax
confused.
          In moonlight, a female
shadow is entering herself. No. The male
is emerging from fate all alone. Have you
ever heard a woman bayoneting a bear?
A man weep in a maternity ward?
The mustache-and-lingerie-wearing sphinx
inside both of us thinks women
are always cock-blocking the apocalypse.
She straps on a cattle prod
and chuckles with her fellow
guards holding cameras and phones. The whore
moaning in a hood on bloody cement
unsheathes his hidden janbiya,
readies the blade. Odds are strangers
have assaulted multiple bodies
still cowering in your DNA. Bodies burning
past their future saints scheduled
to inspire millions of souls. It's time
to revise the myth of purity
and innocence; the myth there can be
no peace without war. Of course,

the me in we loves to ennoble myself;
loves to believe the human spirit always grows.
Yet the sage inside every child knows
in searching for the other: the woman
inside the man inside the animal, you find
truth, lies, and jealous rumors.
                                        Still, at least one man
enshrined in me is reluctant to track down
his most she-wolf self. Several women in him are waiting
for their sons to finally grow
some teeth and move out of the basement.
No. She can't ponder a thing, is too busy walking past
a broken streetlamp. Meanwhile, the man
in my body watches through curtains
a new, larger army, and questions
what all the girls will think if he doesn't volunteer.
No. He's listening
to his sisters already in uniform curse
the end of gender, sex, race, and God as a machine
pumps their milk.
                                There is a woman
and a man naked inside me
who have yet to fully uncleave.
This was long ago, before an abundance
of oxygen. Both reincarnated a wild
bestiary of beings over eons, but this
remained constant: the woman loved
when all the fathers inside all their grandmothers inside all
their grandchildren harmonized into songs
of sadness, joy, tribulations; loved
when, each time, without fail, two lovers
danced to any proscribed border's edge, clutching
their books and musical instruments, breathing
softly through all their most secret sins.
                                        Meanwhile, the old ones
searched for their teeth made of wood, acrylic, gold
in a rose bush under wild mistletoe.
And to long for every girl's laughter was to fly.
And to fly was for every boy's seeking never having to hide.
There is a language within the man I am—dying
at different speeds, the language

an ocean, the human a sea whose
tributaries like frost on a window or vines
on a wall only sometimes in places cross.
I'm looking at one right now
as the child I used to be. Or
are they the veins in my mother's
womb. Or diffuse red
emissions from a cosmos too far away
to revise anything on this evening
but my father's iron
-ed burial clothes.

Ed Bok Lee is the author of, most recently, *Mitochondrial Night*. Lee's poetry has been translated into French, Italian, Spanish, Korean, and Chinese. Honors include an American Book Award, an Asian American Literary Award (Members' Choice Award), a Minnesota Book Award, and a PEN/Open Book Award, among others. With a background in local journalism and political theater, he currently teaches at Metro State University in Minneapolis/St. Paul.

Mari L'Esperance

SOMETHING COMING APART

02-11-2013

In the house
where too much has happened
a boy is dreaming
of resurrection.
He builds it piece
by piece, builds
the possibility of it,
the die-cut components he carefully removes
from their plastic frame,
then glues together, holding them steady.
It is painstaking work.
He is bent over the table
in the dim half-light,
the small shoulders, the dark head dipped
in concentration.
He works steadily
for hours. He works steadily for days
with little sleep, eating when he can.
At last it rises from the clutter,
the airplane with its body gull-white
and sleek,
honed
to a single purpose.

The boy, now older,
lies in a room stinking
of sedatives and sour sheets,
air that's been enclosed for too long.
Outside it is daylight. Students crisscross
a wide lawn littered
with dead leaves.
He is awake, but does not speak,
the same small shoulders, the dark head turned
toward the wall. He has been like this
for days, sleeping a lot, eating when he can.
When I got the call the doctor said
someone

would have to come quickly,
that arrangements would have to be made.
They'd found him on the top floor
of the science building, where the windows
are permanently sealed, standing
for hours
as the dreary gulls circled
the parking lot below,
looking for garbage.

Upstairs in the infirmary guest room
the narrow bed is too hard. I lie awake
for hours. I lie awake for days.

Earlier I overheard the nurse asking:
Where is the mother? The father?

Something fails to translate. Something
is coming apart as I speak.

The huge moon looming outside
my window is too brilliant. It hurts me.

My brother, tell me how we failed you.

Distance creates space to be. If we think of the poem as a living organism that breathes and pulses in the space between poet and reader, it's important to give it just enough attention, but also plenty of room so that its mystery, which is its power, is protected (big for me). In much of (what's popularly known as first-person "confessional" poetry), I find the too-close immediacy of the speaker's experience can feel claustrophobic, suffocating. Which is, of course, where diction, line breaks, white space, even persona-in other words, craft!-help to provide necessary distance and containment. Again, too much distance and you've lost your reader, stamped out the poem's heart. There's also the issue of mining autobiography as material for poetry, which is fine to do, and we all do it, but the question is, how are you going to transform it so that it speaks in a universal way?

Mari L'Esperance's collection *The Darkened Temple* (University of Nebraska Press) was awarded a Prairie Schooner Book Prize in Poetry. An earlier collection, *Begin Here*, was awarded a Sarasota Poetry Theatre Press Chapbook Prize. With Tomás Q. Morín, she co-edited *Coming Close: Forty Essays on Philip Levine* (Prairie Lights Books/U of Iowa Press).

Raina León

BANNED PORTRAIT IN THE MAGA ERA: STUDY SAYS BLACK GIRLS ARE "LESS INNOCENT"

01-24-2023

i opened the door and flipped the black lock
of the clear plastic screen with the framing leaves in stained glass
and out into our postage stamp yard

sun-dancing dandelions
yellow heads and the white for wishing
i was making a bouquet for my mother

my father upstairs in the grips of a peace
that comes only after a 16-hour shift in detention
with boys to whom he never showed my picture

it was a boy passing on a tricycle
his mother far behind
that made me rush in fear

back into the house
i wasn't supposed to be seen unguarded
not presentable and perfect

lock
lock
and down

to the basement for more spring bounty
blush tea roses under the tree bursting
cherry to color a world in petal pink

to go there i had to climb a tall shelf
to find the keys
hidden from little hands

three locks one creaky

method of a child's escape? double-handed body
weight hang to turn the key

barefooted i crept out
careful of fallen pointed branch stubs
to snip and slip in my frayed chemise

a satin basket for all the flowers
then back in and lock the three
and up the stairs

to nestle under my father's arm
that smelled
of roasted onion sweat

already the flowers had wilted
i threw them away when i woke
no one noticed the ruin

Raina J. León, PhD is Black, Afro-Boricua, and from Philadelphia (Lenni Lenape ancestral lands). She is a mother, daughter, sister, madrina, comadre, partner, poet, writer, and teacher educator. She believes in collective action and community work, the profound power of holding space for the telling of our stories, and the liberatory practice of humanizing education. She seeks out communities of care and craft and is a member of the Carolina African American Writers Collective, Cave Canem, CantoMundo, Macondo. She is the author of *black god mother this body*, *Canticle of Idols*, *Boogeyman Dawn*, *sombra : (dis)locate*, and the chapbooks, *profeta without refuge* and *Areyto to Atabey: Essays on the Mother(ing) Self*. She publishes across forms in visual art, poetry, nonfiction, fiction, and scholarly work. She has received fellowships and residencies and attended retreats with The Watering Hole, the Obsidian Foundation, Community of Writers, Montana Artists Refuge, Macdowell, Kimmel Harding Nelson Center for the Arts, Vermont Studio Center, the Tyrone Guthrie Center in Annamaghkerrig, Ireland and Ragdale, among others. She is a founding editor of *The Acentos Review*, an online quarterly, international journal devoted to the promotion and publication of Latinx arts. She is a recipient of a National Association of Latino Arts and Cultures Grant. She recently retired early as a full professor of education at Saint Mary's College of California, only the third Black person (all Black women) and the first Afro-Latina to achieve that rank there. She currently supports poets and writers at the Stonecoast MFA at the University of Southern Maine. She is additionally a digital archivist, emerging visual artist, writing coach, and curriculum developer.

Hugh Martin
MI6A2 ASSAULT RIFLE

03-15-2016

Some days I clean the rifle so it shines,
a cold slice of darkness in grease-stained hands.
Some days, I hate to take it outside, dust
blowing faster, eating the morning brown.
Some days, after the warm silhouettes bow
across the green field of the firing range,
I sit against sandbags, sweat in sunlight,
and hold that grip, the muzzle's edge resting
across the top of my thigh. And some days,
when I've cleaned it for hours, I want only
to take it home for the space of blue wall
above the mantel, because it'd be wrong
to shoot again, to smear and smudge with whorls,
to blemish a thing that makes the night blush.

A veteran of the Iraq War and a former Wallace Stegner Fellow, Hugh Martin is the author of the poetry collections *In Country* and *The Stick Soldiers*. A finalist for a National Magazine Award, Martin's work has appeared in many magazines including *The Atlantic*, *The New Yorker*, *The New York Times*, *GQ*, and *The Sun*.

David Tomas Martinez

TATTLETALE

Don't be a pussy
                        they said
Suck it up
                    they told me
Like a man
                they repeated

until *walk it off, it's only
a scratch, I'll give you something
to cry about* became a simple
tourniquet. As a toddler,

stitches closed shut my scalp.
I hung from a dog's mouth,
flaccid as a rooster's wattle.
I was mauled. Still scarred by
teeth. Like any good secret,

I was carried for only so long.
Eventually after trauma
you're expected to laugh, build
a birdhouse, collect stamps.

I used to have to get drunk,
watch *Twilight or When Harry
Met Sally* to cry. A name

contains destiny and history.
My name means beloved
but some things can't be
loved. Liar, liar teepee

and pants on fire, all my
Yaqui beads traded. Nick

nack paddy wack, dogs
fight over the bone. *Weewee*,
Piggy cried all the way home.

Memory nips my head. *Hush*
lil baby. What punctures child
hood quicker than being
bathroomed, whispered to
suck it.

David Tomas Martinez is the author of two collections of poetry, *Hustle* (2014)
and *Post Traumatic Hood Disorder* (2018), both from Sarabande Books. Martinez is a
Pushcart winner, CantoMundo fellow, a Breadloaf Stanley P. Young fellow, Verlaine
Poetry Award winner, NEA poetry fellow and NEA Big Book author. Martinez lives
in Brooklyn.

Khaled Mattawa

MALOUK'S QASSIDA

03-23-2021

Lampedusa only a dozen leagues now, the bay
between it and Sousse a corridor of debris,
a Phoenician graveyard.

Are we prepared for the storm's paradise?
The starlings recite the zodiacs on their wings;
the marabouts must in kindness abide.

On the wireless the noises of rescue—
the double dealing of virtue and abuse—
into a theater of salvation we ride.

We are exalted into some hippopotamus,
our mouths checked, hands gloved within
human skin, their fingers inside.

The mouths that speak are covered like the Tuaregs',
their eyes swathed with a dusky mirage.
Our names taken, flicker like fireflies.

Looped around our wrists numbers
that look like a kind of price.
The bullhorns cry, the seagulls deride.

On slippery bridges, we're wrapped in gold foil,
woozy, often diseased. But who is saving whom?
The question's not stated, only implied.

Khaled Mattawa was born in Benghazi, Libya, in 1964 and immigrated to the United States in his teens. Mattawa received a BA in political science and economics from the University of Tennessee at Chattanooga before earning an MA in English and an MFA in creative writing from Indiana University, as well as a PhD from Duke University in 2009.

Mattawa's collections of poetry include *Fugitive Atlas* (Graywolf Press, 2020); *Tocqueville* (New Issues, 2010); *Amorisco* (Ausable, 2008); *Zodiac of Echoes* (Ausable, 2003); and *Ismailia Eclipse* (Sheep Meadow Press, 1995). He is also the author of the critical work *Mahmoud Darwish: The Poet's Art and His Nation* (Syracuse University Press, 2014).

Donovan McAbee

MAMA'S BODY

10-20-2025

i. *2004*

The nurses remove the IV,
take the tube from your nose,
move the bed to the center of the room,
so we can circle and pray.

Your spirit, because I believe
on this day in such a thing,
has abandoned its husk, lifted
from the room, or walked out the door.

The marriage of body and breath
broken— Mama   not-Mama
Mama   my first home

ii. *1960*

You woke to the sound of a vase
toppling off an end table—
ran down the hallway
to the door of the living room,
where your Mama lay on the floor,
your Daddy standing above her,
calling her names you were told
not to repeat. You ran
to your room, like you always did.

Years later, you tell me
you'd cover your body
in the sheets, pull the blanket
over your head, close
your eyes and pray to

131

disappear, that the mattress
might swallow you like the ocean.

iii. *1966*

Some things better
left unsaid, so you thought
for two-and-a-half decades,
while those secrets nursed dreams
that crawled through your nights—

how after supper, your friend's Dad
would play strip poker
with you and her at the dining room
table when you were eleven,
how he'd take you later from the bed
where you slept, your friend's Mom

always in the kitchen washing up

iv. *1977*

You at twenty-two
sit on the couch, rubbing
your belly. You hold the little
yellow dress with white
frills that Grandma gave you.

Twenty weeks along,
the ultrasound's silent scan—
Daddy takes you to the hospital,
where the doctor delivers
the stillborn, carries it away.

Two years later,
you put the yellow dress
on me, so you could imagine
how beautiful your little girl
might have been.

v. *1985*

I nuzzle into you
on the couch, rest
in the crook your legs make
as you lie on your side. You stroke
my curly hair, and I go
to sleep, while you and Daddy
watch TV.

You carry me then, down
the hallway, to my bedroom, sing
an ocean lullaby, tuck me in
snug-as-a-bug for the night.

vi. *1993*

You reach out for me, while we drive down 26,
put your hand on my knee, like you've always done—

I draw back, refuse touch. You reach out
with your words to ask about my week, to find out

if there's some girl who's caught my eye. You make
this 350-mile round trip twice every other weekend—

more often when I ask you to, just to see me.

After the divorce, I fortify myself, won't let you

touch me. Won't let Dad touch me.

Don't want to let anyone touch me ever again.

vii. *2001*

Your arm bandaged to keep edema
from settling in. You retch into the plastic
pail the nurse gave you, a reaction
to the anesthesia. You apologize again
for the inconvenience this has caused me,
as I look at the wound under your arm,
where the surgeon removed the lymph nodes.
I take you, next morning, back to the house
to wait for pathology to give us the verdict,
not breast cancer, as everyone has told us,
but melanoma—that word (melanoma) we hear
(melanoma) spread through (melanoma) every
word (melanoma) we speak (melanoma) those
three (melanoma) last (melanoma) years.

viii. *years later*

A need is never sufficient
for its own fulfillment,

or perhaps therein resides
a miracle worth pondering:

an unloved woman
learned to love.

You made water from thirst,
bread from hunger.

ix. *date uncertain*

there must have
been moments
when it felt
like yours

when it didn't belong
to fear or pain
or to a man
or a child

times when your
long dark hair
brushed your shoulders
on a windy day

when the sun
warmed your skin
and you felt the glory
of this other belonging

Donovan McAbee is a poet, songwriter, and essayist. His work has appeared in *The New York Times*, *TIME* magazine, *The Hudson Review*, *The Sun Magazine* (US), *Garden & Gun*, *Poetry London*, and a variety of other places. His poetry chapbook, *Sightings*, was released as part of the Floodgate Series, Vol 7. His academic monograph *Charles Simic and the Poetics of Uncertainty* was published in 2020. He grew up in a small town in South Carolina, in the foothills of the Blue Ridge Mountains. He holds a Master of Divinity degree from Princeton Theological Seminary and a PhD in Creative Writing and Contemporary Poetry from the University of St Andrews in Scotland. Donovan lives in Nashville, Tennessee with his wife and their two children. His poetry collection *Holy the Body* is set to be released by Texas Review Press in 2026.

Nathan McClain

"FIRE DESTROYS BELOVED CHICAGO BAKERY"

12-15-2020

How is it that you misread "fire"
as "father"—your father—
come back from the dead,

to sweep, like hard wind, through the building,
to smash, with a Louisville Slugger,
every pastry with which you'd pack

your sweet little mouth, then
flick a lit match into the trash bin?
The entire building

will have to be demolished
because the father took hours
finally to be put out;

it was a stubborn father. Your father
who once, outside a grocery store,
warned you against asking

for anything inside, so you have learned
to keep your appetites a secret.
And how good you are: refusing,

in the drive thru, the hot apple pie
(two for a dollar), choosing
the house salad over french fries.

But maybe this is why
they all leave you, why you can't
let him rest in peace. The real question is

not why your father would do such a thing,
but why you smell him in every ruin, every
smoldering heap of ash and brick?

Nathan McClain is the author of *Scale* (Four Way Books, 2017) and *Previously Owned* (Four Way Books, 2022), a recipient of fellowships from The Frost Place, Sewanee Writers' Conference, Bread Loaf Writers' Conference, and a graduate of the MFA Program for Writers at Warren Wilson. A Cave Canem fellow, his poems and prose have recently appeared or are forthcoming in *Poetry Northwest*, *Green Mountains Review*, *Zocalo Public Square*, *The Critical Flame*, and *On the Seawall*, among others. He teaches at Hampshire College and serves as Poetry Editor for *The Massachusetts Review*.

Campbell McGrath

PICASSO (1937)

11-24-2015

The canvas that yawns against a wall as blank as Guernica.
The hand that guides the brush that seeks a form.
The name of the town toward which the bombers dove: Guernica.
Cattle on green hillsides, sheep in flocks above Guernica.
a wall   a city   a ruin   a trope   a painting
For the fist and sickle, for the brotherhood of the republic: *Guernica.*
Against the triumph of lies, against the darkness: *Guernica.*
What painter, what artist, what other man than I, Picasso,
could create such a work, duly signed by my hand: *Picasso.*
As for Spain, as for politics, I have stood mute until Guernica,
watching from the safety of exile the tragedy of civil war.
Now, with paints and brushes, I march to war.

a flag   a tyrant   a lamp   the eye of god   a war
The name the lightning burns into our hearts: Guernica.
Let it stand as admonition and animadversion to all war.
Let it serve as totem and reproof to the idiocy of war
as the painting I so name bears witness to its modern form,
to Franco's savagery, the death of innocents, to war
in its ruthless, mechanical guise, 20th Century war, total war.
Against the bombs of the Fascists I counterpose my painting.
Against the destruction of Spain and its people, let this painting
embody the tribute and testament of Pablo Picasso.
The name of the matador and the name of the bull: Picasso.

The name of the minotaur, the name of the tauromach: Picasso.
The name of the enemy and his implement: war.
Against which, like the thunderbolts of Zeus, Picasso
hurls paint against canvas, creation against death: *yo, Picasso!*
From the blue sky, by the hundreds, bombs falling on Guernica.
oil paint   the eye of god   a sword   a scream   Picasso
a candle   a memory   a dream   the world in flames   Picasso
Mothers bearing dead children are anguish given form.
Stink of burned flesh and wool is obliteration in animal form.

In the eye of the bull, in the scream of the horse: Picasso.
In art there can be no compromise; only while painting
can I perceive what transcends the historical act of painting.

a lance   a banner   a template   an annunciation   a painting
A brush is a weapon of vengeance in the hand of Picasso,
to strike down death-merchants, haters of modern painting,
Franco, Mussolini, Hitler with his sentimental flower paintings.
"If cities are destroyed from the air, the enemy cannot carry on the war.
The annihilation of Guernica resembles a victorious painting
by an old master, not this infantile, degenerate painting."
From failure, from breakage, from silence, from loss: *Guernica*.
The name of the dove in the burning dovecote: Guernica.
a vision   a wound   a flame a teardrop   a painting
With pencil, with chalk, with a brush I shall seek its form—
with my hands I shall remodel what tyranny deforms.

As for Spain, lost to medieval slumber, to a violent form
of self-abnegation, like an apparition from a Goya painting
she sinks again into the darkness. Power is a form
of narcissism; totalitarianism corrupts even as it informs
those who destroy and those who create, both Franco and Picasso.
In a century to which devastation has given its true form
Guernica is an elemental dispensation, a document formed
in the name of humanity to denounce the nightmare of war.
Against chaos, against ignorance, against all future war
a brush moves across canvas and truth takes the form
of Dresden, of Nanking, of Hiroshima, of Guernica.
The name of the burning world is Guernica.

a vigil   a vessel   a fist   a pyre   a form
a plume   a banner   a vision   a trope   a painting
a veil   a scream   a wound   the world in flames   Picasso
a tyrant   an elegy   a lamp   a dove   a war
a dream   a ruin   a teardrop   the eye of god   Guernica

Born in Chicago to Irish-Catholic parents, Campbell McGrath earned a BA from the University of Chicago and an MFA from Columbia University. Influenced by Walt Whitman, James Wright, Sylvia Plath, and Rainer Maria Rilke, McGrath writes predominantly free verse, long-lined, documentary poems deeply engaged with American popular culture and commerce. A master of the long poem, he has also written many prose poems as well as shorter lyrics. McGrath has published numerous collections of poetry, including *Fever of Unknown Origin* (Knopf, 2023); *Nouns & Verbs: New and Selected Poems* (2019); and *Spring Comes to Chicago* (1996), which won the Kingsley Tufts Poetry Award. In awarding the prize, poet Garrett Hongo labeled McGrath's unique tone "ironic romanticism." The centerpiece of the collection, and one of McGrath's best-known poems, is "The Bob Hope Poem," a 70-page opus modeled on Robert Pinsky's "An Explanation of America" and James McMichael's "Four Good Things." In a 2005 interview McGrath explained that the poem's shape "is not a narrative but a symphonic structure."

Shivani Mehta

THE MUSEUM

01-26-2016

I was thirteen the first time I visited the Museum of Breezes, with my Grandfather who was eighty-three. Housed in a stone mansion and founded in 1827, it boasts one thousand and seventy-three different species of breezes caught from around the world and categorized into sections by strength, according to the Wheeler-Yoshida scale.[1] The first section contains light summer winds, thin wisps of silk, clear and colorless in their glass jars stacked in even rows. In the slant of wintery afternoon light, the jars looked empty. I had to squint to catch the swirls before they vanished. The next section houses medium strength winds collected from cooler climates in the Northern hemisphere. These are wetter, like breezes after rain. Thick and murky, so heavy they sink to the bottom of their jars where they pool like grey mists in an open field. Grandfather said their stillness reminded him of the war, the time he crawled on his belly for miles, the weight of the sky pressing down like an old mattress. Lastly, cordoned off in a section by themselves are the storm winds, the squalls, gales, typhoons, hurricanes. These are the heaviest of all, thick and opaque, each imprisoned in its own shatter-proof glass cage, six inches thick to muffle their screams.

Shivani Mehta's second book, *The Required Assembly*, is from Press 53 in 2025. She is also the author of *Useful Information for the Soon-to-be Beheaded*. Her poems have appeared in many literary journals. Born in Mumbai, Shivani grew up in Singapore. A former attorney, she lives in Los Angeles with her husband and two children, where she co-owns and manages a business.

---

1 The Wheeler-Yoshida scale for cataloguing breezes according to their weight was developed in the early 1800s by British meteorologist Mina Wheeler and Japanese climatologist, B.C. Yoshida.

Wayne Miller
A PRAYER (O CITY—)

04-30-2012

O arrow landed deep in Harold's eye—

O voice
pressing upward against the sky—

O light and steam.

(When the western windows
of the City go pink, the rooms behind them
lock shut with clouds.)

O clouds—

   (Slipping down in the morning
to part around the skyrises, to marble
the rooftop shanties and gardens,
the hammocks and clotheslines.)

And graying water tanks—

 (Our water lifted
into the clouds—and me, drawing it
down into my cup, my breath
pressed to the shimmering surface.)

O City—

 (That breathes itself
into the glass—that pulls me to the window
I press my gaze through,
I press my face to—)

O City—

142

(And the makers,
who drew the City through the membranes
of paper and canvas,
giving the city to the City—)

  O City—

(And our tables and demitasses,
woofers and fire escapes,
kisses in doorways, weapons
and sculptures, concerts
and fistfights, sex toys and votives,
engines and metaphors—.)

City of Joists—

(The City shot through with them.)

City of Doorways—
  (The City opens us,
and we step through.)

O Light-Coming-on-in-a-Window—

(Since you've opened the fridge,
opened your book, opened your room
to the room next door.)

O City—
(Pushing through the dark
like the nose of a plane.)

O City—
(It could be a bomber,
night-black, the instruments on auto,
the pilot asleep in his lounger.)

O City—
(In the hull below, words
are written on the bombs in Sharpie.)

———

(There's also a folder of letters lying off to the side in the dark.

In one of them, the pilot's brother describes some fingerprints he's found pressed inside the lip of a broken jar.

He's an archeologist. The prints are from the jar's maker—just after the Battle of Hastings, near the end of the eleventh century.)

Wayne Miller is the author of six poetry collections, most recently *The End of Childhood* (Milkweed Editions, 2025) and *We the Jury* (2021). His awards include the UNT Rilke Prize, two Colorado Book Awards, an NEA Translation fellowship, a Pushcart Prize, six individual awards from the Poetry Society of America, and a fulbright to the Seamus Heaney Centre in Northern Ireland. He teaches at the University of Colorado Denver, co-directs the Unsung Masters Series, and edits *Copper Nickel*.

Deborah A. Miranda

HOW TO LOVE THE BURNING WORLD

04-14-2021

> *…is it still possible to face the gathering darkness, and say to the physical Earth, and to all its creatures, including ourselves, fiercely and without embarrassment, I love you, and to embrace fearlessly the burning world?*
> —Barry Lopez

Tell yourself it's like sitting at the bedside
of your mother; scorched with cancer,
her hand already almost ash in yours,
her words already smoke so thick
it obscures your vision of a future
without her. You want to look away.
You want to find a cave, drink yourself
into oblivion, sleep while ugliness smolders.
Admit it. You want someone else to tend
the deathwatch. Instead, moisten her tongue
with a sponge; bathe dry skin
with lavender cream; braid her hair
with tender, trembling fingers. Take care
not to pull on knots. Stay in the room:
let the last thing she hears
be your voice, thanking her
for every single time she didn't
kill you, for the eons she waited
before you realized her brilliance,
her wisdom, all the days she bit
her tongue, let you think you had
the last bloody word.

You aren't required to love the flames.

But love the burning world.
You owe her that. Fear is no dishonor.
Her fever so hot even metaphors
melt at a touch. Memorize her.

Praise each scar on her body,
beauty ablaze. Pray for a clean
ending, a phoenix purification.
Pray for mercy. Pray for the only thing
that can save us now:
every lesson she ever taught us
about the sweet, bitter grace
of transformation.

Deborah A. Miranda is an enrolled member of the Ohlone-Costanoan Esselen Nation, with Santa Ynez Chumash ancestry. She is author of *Bad Indians: A Tribal Memoir*, four poetry collections and is finishing a fifth collection, *maxana chempapisi: Blood Writing*. Former Thomas H. Broadus Professor of English at Washington and Lee University, she now lives in Eugene, Oregon.

Juan J. Morales

A GOOD EDUCATION

03-01-2016

As a girl in Ecuador, my mother recited saints, prayers, and science formulas.
Our reports in Social Studies did the same when we studied places like
Ecuador and commonwealths like Puerto Rico,

served up imports, exports, populations, lags in class with poster board
markered and spilled glue.

The world's violence fell from minds like pencils dropped under ancient
radiators.

It's all about patriotism learned in a classroom, my mother admiring the
Incan King Atahualpa and shaking her head at brother Huáscar.

Lessons widened the divide with Peru, the other country.

Amazing how civil war boils between brothers, flaring up battlegrounds no
one can pinpoint.

The blame game helped my mom and her class imagine the disputed zone, el
oriente, that divides two countries, that bends young, confused thoughts that
clamped inside her, tight fists balled in pride.

And I put myself there too,

getting a good education, oblivious to our country's failings, saying the pledge
of allegiance and gawking up at the flag with my small hand on my heart,
about which

I knew nothing.

Juan J. Morales is the son of an Ecuadorian mother and Puerto Rican father and grew up in Colorado. He is the author of four poetry collections, including *The Handyman's Guide to End Times* and his latest, *Dream of the Bird Tattoo*, published University of New Mexico Press. Morales has received fellowships from CantoMundo, Macondo, Longleaf Writers Conference, and he has served as the editor/publisher of Pilgrimage Press. He lives in Pueblo, Colorado and is an Assistant Professor of English at Colorado College.

John Murillo

DISTANT LOVER
(OR, WHEN YOU'RE TEACHING IN AMHERST AND,
WHILE ON A LATE NIGHT WALK, YOUR WIFE CALLS
FROM BROOKLYN TO SAY GOODNIGHT)

12-1-2020

The dead of February, and everything
sexual. So sexual the icicles skirting the
barn.
Sexual the animals huddled inside,
shivering. Sexual the cloud disappearing,
appearing again, from your half-open
mouth. The moon swollen bright. Sexual the
trees, stark
naked, all their branches spread and
undulating in the wind. Sexual the tundra.
Sexual
the blackest snow by the road, made blacker
by the city worker's plow. Sexual, the
snowman leaning in a midnight yard. So
sexual
dead February, the small town windows lit
from inside, fogging, watching you burn.

John Murillo is the author of the poetry collections *Up Jump the Boogie* (Cypher
2010, Four Way Books 2020), finalist for both the Kate Tufts Discovery Award and
the Pen Open Book Award, and *Kontemporary Amerikan Poetry* (Four Way 2020),
winner of the Kingsley Tufts Poetry Award and the Poetry Society of Virginia's
North American Book Award, and finalist for the PEN/Voelcker Award for Poetry,
Believer Poetry Award, Maya Angelou Book Award, Hurston/Wright Foundation
Legacy Award and the NAACP Image Award. His other honors include the Four
Quartets Prize from the T.S. Eliot Foundation and the Poetry Society of America,
two Larry Neal Writers Awards, a pair of Pushcart Prizes, the J Howard and
Barbara MJ Wood Prize from the Poetry Foundation, an NYSCA/NYFA Artist
Fellowship, and fellowships from the National Endowment for the Arts, the Bread
Loaf Writers Conference, Fine Arts Work Center in Provincetown, Cave Canem
Foundation, and the Wisconsin Institute for Creative Writing. Murillo's poems have
appeared in such publications as *American Poetry Review*, *Poetry*, and *Best American
Poetry 2017, 2019*, and *2020*. Currently, he is an associate professor of English and
director of the creative writing program at Wesleyan University.

Frank Paino

ROUGH ALCHEMY

08-29-2025

(Fiji Mermaid—Destroyed in Kimball Museum Fire,
Boston, circa 1880)

Hardly a seductress, you were ruined
the moment some cruel dreamer stitched you together

in the creaking bowels of a South Pacific fishing boat,
a thing conjured from savage diminution—one striped mackerel

snatched from its deep cerulean life, scaled back to dorsal fin
and caudal taper, one hapless monkey suddenly missing

everything below her delicate waist. Mermaid. Creature
of sleeplessness, withered breasts that could suckle nothing

but the benthic cold of ocean rifts, who might have dared
to kiss your mouthful of daggered teeth? Still, they paid

by the thousands to stand in the half-light until pupils went wide
enough to summon your twisted form, arms drawn up

as if in wonder, malignant lips stretched in the eternal O
of your rictus. But what was it they wanted to see if not

what they did not want to see? Like the man who staggers
from a bombed-out building beneath the swizzled light of tracers,

eyes fixed on nothing but the place his right hand used to be,
even though he knows it's useless, knows what's left

of those elegant fingers still rests on the Steinway's shattered
keyboard three stories and a sudden world away,

just as his body, in years to come, will refuse
to accept the loss of its song, will trace a spectral twin

under Kirlian light sapphire as Chernobyl's half-life
until he comes to believe that insistent, luminous print

is a small voice crying out from a ruined city,
the wild prophet of a promised reunion that waits somewhere

beyond his terminal breath. And who among us could refuse
such rough alchemy, a world beyond what merely seems:

mortar rounds breaking twenty-seven bones against eighty-eight
wooden keys, but only for so long. Or you, misshapen offspring

of ocean and earth, rising from the inferno's crucible, no longer
monstrous, but something beautiful. Something bright.

Frank Paino's fourth book, *Dark Octaves*, was just published by Longleaf Press. His chapbook, *Pietà*, won the Jacar Press Chapbook Prize and was published in 2023. He has received a Pushcart Prize, The Cleveland Arts Prize in Literature, and an Individual Excellence Award from the Ohio Arts Council. His website is: www.frankpaino.net

Gregory Pardlo

WINTER AFTER THE STRIKE

06-22-2007

You believe,
if you cast wide enough

your net of want and will, something meaningful
will respond. Perhaps we are the response—

each a cresting echo hesitating, vibrant with the moment
before rippling back.

But you're steadfast as Odysseus strapped to the mast, as you were
in '81 when Reagan ordered you back to work. You were President

of the union local you steered with your working-man's voice,
the voice that ground the Ptolemaic ballet of air traffic to
  a temporary stop.

You used it to refuse to cross the picket line I walked
with you outside Newark International.

I miss sitting beside you at the console when you worked
graveyard shift in the tower. Mom and I visited with our
  sleeping bags.

I could see the dark Turnpike for miles, the somber
office buildings winking insomniac cells, the tarmac

spread before us like a picnic blanket and you, like a jade Buddha
suffused in the glow of that radial EKG.

You'd push the microphone in front of me, nod, and let me
  give the word.
I called all my stars home, trajectories bent on the weight
  of my voice.

You say you miss tracking those leviathans, each one snagged
  on the barb
of your liturgy. I, too, get reeled in by the hard, now rusty music
  of your pipes.

I follow it back to the day of your accident in the story you tell:
you were sixteen, hurdling the railings dividing row-house porches

from one end of Widener Place to the other to impress Mom.
I imagine the way you cleared each one like a leaf bobbing
  on water, catching

the penultimate, the rubber toe of your Chuck Taylors kissed
by the rail, upsetting your rhythm and you roiled in the air
  headlong,

arms outstretched, stumbling toward the last like one hell-bent
or sick to the stomach. The way you landed, on your throat,
  the rail

could have taken your head clean off. Since then, your voice issues
like some wartime communiqué: a ragged, typewritten dispatch

which you swallow with your smoker's cough black as a tire
spinning in the snow. That winter after the strike,

we were so poor you sold everything but the house. Tell me, Dad,
when you'd stand at the door calling me in for the night,

could you hear me speaking to snowflakes falling beneath
  the lamppost?
Could you hear me out there, imitating you imitating prayer?

**I don't mean to sound romantic, but I think...[poetry] is on some
level either an act of resistance, if merely against its own diction,
or an act of opposition. Opposition, like prayer, is also celebratory.
Every time I posit an oppositional force, I'm simultaneously
affirming the thing opposed. I think of it in terms of the paternal
relationship: I want to stand independently of my pig-headed**

father, but I don't want to stand alone. (Coincidentally, we can think of many other social relationships in this regard as well.) For example, like many of us, so much of my thought process conforms to the narrative structures of prime time television and Spielberg films. I find this sort of grotesquely fascinating. So while it might seem more literary to claim Whitman or Hopkins as the influence I'm struggling to get from under, my influences are actually quite pedestrian. I'm also engaged in various levels of resistance: resistance to easy categorization, resistance to stereotypes and biased assumptions, resistance to participation in modes of thought that provision forms of social oppression. Resistance entails more subversive maneuvers because I really hope to destabilize the thing in question. The object here is to have the reader challenge her own assumptions about the primacy or even necessity of certain cultural beliefs. I love that moment when some essence of my world cracks open and suddenly there is a whole new spectrum of possibility. A given poem may not cause that crack, but it can certainly compromise the levee.

Gregory Pardlo is a graduate of Rutgers University-Camden. He received an MFA from NYU as a New York Times Fellow in Poetry, an MFA in nonfiction from Columbia University as a Teaching Fellow, and an MPhil from the CUNY Graduate Center. Pardlo is the author of *Digest*, winner of the 2015 Pulitzer Prize for Poetry; *Totem*, winner of the 2007 American Poetry Review / Honickman Prize; and translator from the Danish of Niels Lyngsø's, *Pencil of Rays and Spiked Mace*. *Air Traffic*, a memoir in essays, was published by Knopf in 2018. His most recent book, *Spectral Evidence*, was long listed for the 2024 National Book Award in poetry. His poems and essays have appeared in *The New Yorker*, *Playboy*, *American Poetry Review*, *Boston Review*, *The Nation*, *The New York Times*, *Ploughshares*, *Tin House*, and two editions of *Best American Poetry*, as well as many anthologies including the *Norton Anthology of Contemporary African American Poetry*. He is the recipient of fellowships from the New York Public Library's Cullman Center, the Guggenheim Foundation, the New York Foundation for the Arts, and a fellowship for translation from the National Endowment for the Arts. He has received other fellowships from the Civitella Ranieri Foundation, MacDowell, the Lotos Club Foundation and Cave Canem. Pardlo is Poetry Editor of *Virginia Quarterly Review* and advising editor for *Callaloo*, a journal of African diaspora arts and letters.

Ed Pavlic

MASQUALÉRO

09-28-2007

—after Miles

There's plenty that think we're twins. By 18
  we'd both wished secretly that it was true,
    & that it wasn't. Since we were 9

we met here on stealth banks of August,
  each year another Savior & sweet thanks be
    to Jesus for that old rowboat.

Remember my instructions when we met?
  I'd bent a coffee can into a scoop to hunt
    the mud banks for crawfish. "The whole

trick with blue pinchers is getting in behind
  without setting off a stir on their tail." Now
    we're getting to be His age. But apart

from watches & sky dates, you know how to find me
  when my head's full of scuppernong blossoms.
    So we cast off past wisteria

& into night silk beyond the river's edge. Empty skins
  of tree snakes, ash vibrissa, draw the canopy.
    Tangles of moss wisp past my cheeks,

fall out of a lullaby. No moon. If I spark my lighter,
  willows young & old pretend they don't breathe
    the dark, don't slip thru nights

in tangos with cypress & Saturn tuned in to bent
  underwater reeds. Posed they stand like a big-city
    crowd at a bust stop, & just reach

off the bank for elbow room. Come out that white blouse
  & upside down, you watch open lilies fall away,
    a bird's eye vision

of your daddy's parachute into the Mekong Delta.
  A back bend arched over the bow, your bare torso slips
    thru a summer breeze, cuts

a hush in the cicada din. A pale gash torn past my lips
  leaves the night open. Light-plays off my chrome
    Zippo. Hershey's kisses harden

into rose thorns dense as a shut eye's faith in tarot.
  My name, dry salt on an arch-smooth eyebrow,
    vanishes into steamed woods & gut-heavy

air like sweat into a prayer for rain. We take on water
  in each Decatur Street groan for Mercy. It's far too late,
    slipway a damned sight too steep

for Esperanto or one-eyed jacks. To pull the moon
  back with cracked oars curved like tusks, you'd better
    mean it. It's about time for round two.

Oceanus descends with an acetylene tear & dreams
  of a blue tip, a cool flame; the other eye's been gone
    for years, blind & lid turned cold side out.

**A poem exists. One part of a poem exists when it answers a need
in the author. Something has to happen while writing, out of bolt-
blue, that answers a question that didn't exist in the mind until
the answer identified it. Another part of a poem exists when that
accident in the author's body answers something in the need of a
reader. I think readers and writers both come to poetry out of a
need distinct from the ways we approach various kinds of prose. I
think we come to it closer to the way musicians and listeners come
to music or the way a painter and a viewer approach a canvas.**

Poems are made of language held in tension with its non-verbal properties. When an experience can be made to speak, when it can be literally voiced, in a way that opens it up (rather than sums it up) into what's behind it, into what surrounds it, that can last I think. It's similar to what makes a song seem to mean more than what the story of the words tell. I think that lasts, but it can't be requisitioned or controlled. It's in the way one can instantly come to depend on the results of an accident. The best parts of poems are the results of the right accidents.

Ed Pavlić (Ph. D. Indiana University) is Distinguished Research Professor of English and African American Studies and affiliated faculty in Creative Writing. Pavlić's 13 published books range across (and at times between) genres: poetry, non-fiction, critical studies, and a novel.

Monica Prince

THREE SCENES FROM *ROADMAP: A CHOREOPOEM*

09-15-2025

At eleven, I cut myself on a razor someone left in the bathroom sink.
My mother was asleep. It wasn't her razor. It felt good—
at first. Then slithered in shame. I'm not supposed
to like this. But cutting helped me disappear
into the whiteness preferred of me.

But not by my mother—who, most days,
loved this country. She never taught me
to hate the police or burn flags,
but when it came to existing while Black,
she asked me to hold still, never raise my voice.

In college, my Black professor warned me of a KKK sect
rooted at the edge of town. There, I added
rope to my list of bodily fears, after *water, white hoods,*
and *trees.* I do not trust any person that wears hate
like a badge of honor, masking fear of the other as pride.

Ever since blade released blood from my skin,
I haven't been able to relax my spine in public.
What if someone discovers the trenches I've carved
in my arms, stomach, and hips? Who will tell my mother
her son is a map of every way Black men can die?

Before she passed, my mother was sober. No more clients,
no more strangers leaving razors in the bathroom.
Not that it mattered. By then, highways illuminated my skin,
leading to self-preservation, constantly under construction.
Like her, I worry if naming my child signs their death warrant.

Maybe that's just the risk of having a Black child. I'm not immune
to all the ways the world disrupts my peace, how it burrows
into my cells. But I've since traded razors for needles
filled with ink, drawn pictures on this body to immortalize
the perforations I scratched for whoever comes to tear me apart.

It should be harder to find them now, to separate
my flesh from my blood. Let it be known: innocence
is not the line in the sand for the end of childhood.
As if the worst way to grow up is to be ripped from it,
typically by someone who had theirs ruined, too.

But if we are all refugees of our childhoods,
drifting forever outside of that place, balanced
on the line of innocence and whatever comes next,
I'm not surprised by the moon, dictating
blood and ocean. I'm not even surprised by

what had to be my mother's undoing—a man,
a gun, her skin too dark and her sex
too loud. She tried. I know that's nearly all
I could expect from her, to do and have done her best,
to never identify my remains should I die first.

She got her wish—to never have to mourn her baby
or learn the name of the coward who took him from her.
But now I live without her, my body scarred over
with new melanin, tattoos like liquid bandages keeping me intact,
her memory a promise to never abandon my own kid.

I want to be enough for the child I bring into this suffering,
be able to vow not to smoke
or leave without saying goodbye. I can only hope
I can do it—bring someone here,
trust I won't do more damage.

Dancer enters stage right.

DANCER
Although Black youth have historically not been considered at high
risk for suicide and self-harm, current trends now challenge that. The
Congressional Black Caucus and the Youth Risk Behavior Survey,
developed by the CDC, both reported that Black males are engaging in
more lethal means when attempting suicide. Self-harm is considered
a "white thing," and the stigma around mental health in the Black
community prevents many Black youth from reporting their challenges
with self-harm and suicidal ideation.

Dancer approaches Neil and takes the razor from him, who hands it over at first reluctantly, then resolutely. He nods at the dancer that then exits stage right. Neil remains on stage while Raven enters from the back of the room. While they recite, Raven makes her way to the stage.

RAVEN
Our lives are divided into two parts:
before Dorian, and after.

NEIL
Before Dorian, you were my feel-good.
To call you an escape would cheapen the joy.
Life was always a little enflamed, a series of open wounds
charred at the edges. I learned to stay inside the blood,
where it's warm, where immunity multiplies.

RAVEN
Before Dorian, I wanted stories. You told me once
that love has no rules, just pulsing need.
It's possible to break a heart by accident, to walk away
in the middle out of fear. But you didn't do that.
For five years before Dorian, you didn't leave.

Raven gets on stage and dances with Neil.

NEIL
You're drunk, and it's midnight.
You want stories, so you peel my shirt off,
begging me to show you what ink does to skin,
did to this body. You don't ask why
there are so many tattoos, or what they hide.
I couldn't tell you if you did. Not yet.
To this day, you still ignore my past pain,
believe me stronger than yesterday would suggest.

RAVEN
I'm drunk, and it's midnight.
You want to feel good, so you let me undress you,
slide my painted nails against every image and outline,
my body melting into yours. I cannot tell you
why my orgasms sound like grenades shattering
century-old foundation, don't want you
to imagine me unstable, ruined. I whisper the word
survivor into your collarbone—a promise, a kinship.

NEIL
You lick each syllable, trace each picture
with your pointed tongue, pull the scars right out of me.
We drown in the sticky parts, the urgency of the moment,
what was supposed to be another harmless night turning permanent.

RAVEN
In the morning, I already know we're in the after.

NEIL
My skin wears your name,
and I can't scrub you off.

*Neil and Raven stand together in the
center. Neil rubs his hand over Raven's
belly, and they smile at each other.*

RAVEN
I'll name him Dorian.

NEIL
A gift—from the sea.

RAVEN
Just like his daddy.

NEIL
Just like his legacy.

*Dorian enters at the back of
the room and stays there.*

DORIAN
When it comes to Black families,
the version you expect looks like this:

> *Neil and Raven's body language changes.*
> *Neil looks enraged and she looks scared.*
> *They move away from each other, and*
> *Neil pulls out a flask and starts to drink.*
> *Raven becomes visibly anxious.*

DORIAN
Father's a drunk.
Mother's a coward.

NEIL *(shouting at Raven)*
You don't understand!
Everyone's against the Black man—the white man,
the white woman, you!

RAVEN
Don't you mean the Black woman,
who's always right here?
Standing with you?

NEIL
Standing *on* me!

> *Neil puts the flask back in his pocket*
> *and reaches for Raven. They begin*
> *an abusive dance in the style of the*
> *violent French l'apache, as Neil tries to hit*
> *her but continues to miss while Raven*
> *evades his blows and tries to calm him.*

Poetry proves that replication, imitation, and straight up theft are what make poets magical, what make poets love other poets. I allow myself to break conventions when it comes to form and what poetry "should" look like because someone gave me permission. Ntozake Shange created the choreopoem form—she coined the term in 1975, she put it on Broadway in 1976, and she wrote more choreopoems in response to her own need to never stay still during her poetry readings. Poetry and dance were inseparable to Shange—and with that permission to blow up form, I made poetry, dance, art, music, drama, parkour, nursery rhymes, and more inseparable. When I approached the choreopoem, I thought it was lightning in a bottle. Shange gave silent permission to every Black woman in the world with her choreopoem For colored girls who have considered suicide / when the rainbow is enuf. She said, "Your story is important, your voice matters, your body is necessary." So, generations of us since have written choreopoems not just as tribute, but as a promise fulfilled. When someone gives you permission without you needing to ask, without you even knowing you needed it to begin, your world changes. The choreopoem was my first concrete step into poetry after learning how to slam. I write shows about the vicarious grief I hold for the African diaspora—how hard we fight just to stay alive. We deserve better. Shange showed me how—so I write in her honor to show others how, too.

Monica Prince, associate professor of activist and performance writing, serves as Director of Africana Studies at Susquehanna University in Pennsylvania. She is the author of Roadmap: A Choreopoem, How to Exterminate the Black Woman: A Choreopoem, Instructions for Temporary Survival, and Letters from the Other Woman. Her work appears in Wildness, The Missouri Review, The Texas Review, The Rumpus, MadCap Review, American Poetry Journal, and elsewhere. As one of the foremost choreopoem scholars, Prince writes, teaches, and performs choreopoems across the nation.

Octavio Quintanilla

SONNET FOR HUMAN SMUGGLERS

02-28-2023

Take care of them. If they want water,
    Dump them in the river. If they crave
Freedom, let them loose among rattlesnakes.
    If they want to breathe, let them breathe dust.

Let the desert mouse nest in their white bones.
Give them shelter with your greed. With your rape.

The road kill is a sign you're almost home.
    Point to it and show them who they are.
Their life's a documentary, a newscast.

    But for you, everything is possible.
You're the map that leads them astray,
    Priest leading a funeral procession.

Load this cargo. Shackle them with promises,
    Backaches that keep them from killing you.

Octavio Quintanilla is the author of the poetry collections, *If I Go Missing* (Slough Press, 2014), *The Book of Wounded Sparrows* (Texas Review Press, 2024), which has been longlisted for the American Book Award, and *Las Horas Imposibles / The Impossible Hours*, winner of the 2024 Ambroggio Prize given by the Academy of American Poets, forthcoming from the University of Arizona Press. Octavio is the founder and director of the literature & arts festival, Versofrontera, publisher of Alabrava Press, and former Poet Laureate of San Antonio, TX. His frontextos (visual poems) have been published and exhibited widely. He teaches Literature and Creative Writing at Our Lady of the Lake University. Connect IG: @ writeroctavioquintanilla

Saara Myrene Raapana

SMOKE

04-02-2024

As in:
You can tell the source by its color

If eye-white	Noxzema	cotton swab	
then moisture	or	a freshly burning thing	

and if soup spoon	gypsum	raincloud	key
then Frisbee	Barbie	Matchbox car	

and if lake ice	wrist veins	Zoloft	sky
then Marlboro	pipe	or steamroller	

but if crude oil	midnight	fry-pan	tire
then black fire	steel char	blindrun	gone

As in:
What we steal from Kelly's father
and from our handsy, stingy boyfriends,
we take behind the sauna. We pick, pack, giggle, hiss.
I hide what's left inside my Care Bear's head
so later I can light the snow-soaked tree
that bares its boughs inside me.

As in:
My mother at the sink   ash-sizzle in the whiskey glass
My mother and the curtains drawn   her dark and spinning room

My father   midnight   on the porch alone
his orange-red cherry   visible to everyone

164

As in:
What seeps in or what escapes.
What I blow into a stuffed toilet paper tube,
go tiptoe to release. What seeps ventwise
to the visitation room to stroke
my mother's wrist, her ash-dry hair

As in:
What tells me wind-direction
how quick   how mad

What tells me   –stop–   before I turn the knob

What tells me   –sure   walk through that door
but only if you want to inhale fire–

Born and raised in the Upper Peninsula of Michigan, Saara Myrene Raappana served as a Peace Corps Volunteer in southern China before moving to Southwest Minnesota. She wrote the chapbooks *A Story of America Goes Walking* (in collaboration with artist Rebekah Wilkins-Pepiton (Shechem Press, 2016) and *Milk Tooth, Levee, Fever* (Dancing Girl Press, 2015), and has published sundry poems in journals, anthologies, and very fancy paintings. She's also worked in comparative international education, magazine editing, poetry film, and functional strength. She teaches composition and kettlebells (separately) and co-owns the very best gym, Restored Strength. She's received grants and scholarships from the Minnesota State Arts Board, the Southwest Minnesota Arts Council, and the Sewanee Writers' Conference. She likes ice fishing, train rides, reading poems to rooms full of strangers, and making up new names for imprecisely labelled birds. *Chamber After Chamber* is Saara's first ful-length collection of poetry. Saara passed away on March 27, 2024.

Khalisa Rae

MAD. BLACK. BIRD.

08-16-2022

The caged bird sings
with a fearful trill,
of things unknown,
but longed for still.
—Maya Angelou, "Caged Bird"

A woman walked up; told me I was
beautiful. Eyes stark and mesmerized,
started to lift her hand and lean in to touch
my feather, the crest of my head.

Gawking,
she called her other friends over to pet
and view my exotic, my natural.

And if I had swatted her hand away,
screamed and pushed her, I would have
been called beast, wild animal,
untamed.

How do you cope?

They say,
Can I touch it?
            So wide. Look.
So big, so full.

Can I keep her?

When everyone tells you to hide your true self,
but wearing the features they made you
hate, your body does not know whether to
change its stripes or break the bars and run.

166

It's hard to look in the mirror; to not hear their

voices: *You'd be prettier if you bleached,*

snipped a wing or two,

trimmed the fat,

if your squawk wasn't so riotous.

I am losing myself.

Been here so long, this cage feels more
like a home, More like a place to rest
under, than escape. The more they tell me
to change,
the harder it is to remember what I loved
about myself—my long neck, full beak,
plumage like ink. This beautiful
mahogany tail that spans majestic,
crooked appendix that keeps waving.

Khalisa Rae is an award-winning author, activist, and storyteller. As a queer rights advocate and community builder, she seeks to uplift Black queer voices. She is the author of the poetry collection, Ghost in a Black Girl's Throat and the sold-out play production, Seven Deadly Sins of Being a Woman.

Paisley Rekdal

WHY SOME GIRLS LOVE HORSES

03-04-2013

And then I thought, Can I have more
of this, would it be possible
for every day to be a greater awakening: more light,
more light, your face on the pillow
with the sleep creases rudely
fragmenting it, hair so stiff
from paint and sheet rock it feels
like the dirty short hank
of mane I used to grab on Dandy's neck

before he hauled me up and forward,
white flanks flecked green
with shit and the satin of his dander,
the livingness, the warmth
of all that blood just under the skin
and in the long, thick muscle of the neck-
He was smarter than most of the children
I went to school with. He knew
how to stand with just the crescent
of his hoof along a boot toe and press,
incrementally, his whole weight down. The pain
so surprising when it came,
its iron intention sheathed in stealth, the decisive
sudden twisting of his leg until the hoof
pinned one's foot completely to the ground,
we'd have to beat and beat him with a brush
to push him off, that hot
insistence with its large horse eye trained
deliberately on us, to watch-

Like us, he knew how to announce through violence
how he didn't hunger, didn't want
despite our practiced ministrations: too young
not to try to empathize
with this cunning: this thing
that was and was not human we must respect
for itself and not our imagination of it: I loved him because
I could not love him anymore

in the ways I'd taught myself,
watching the slim bodies of teenagers
guide their geldings in figure eights around the ring
as if they were one body, one fluid motion
of electric understanding I would never feel
working its way through fingers to the bit: this thing
had a name, a need, a personality; it possessed
an indifference that gave me
logic and a measure: I too might stop wanting
the hand placed on back or shoulder
and never feel the desired response.
I loved the horse for the pain it could imagine

and inflict on me, the sudden jerking
of head away from halter, the tentative nose
inspecting first before it might decide
to relent and eat. I loved
what was not slave or instinct, that when you turn to me
it is a choice, it is always a choice to imagine pleasure
might be blended, one warmth
bleeding into another as the future
bleeds into the past, more light, more light,
your hand against my shoulder, the image
of the one who taught me disobedience
is the first right of being alive.

Narrative allows me to explore the psychological aspects of the world I'm trying to describe: to write character, but also to think about story, which I love. But lyric allows me to leap between stories, to move quickly between time periods. I like poems that put the personal event alongside historical events or narratives, and the lyric allows me to move between what might seem like wildly different moments in time and meaning.

Paisley Rekdal is the author of four books of nonfiction and seven collections of poetry, including *Animal Eye*, winner of the UNT Rilke Prize; *Imaginary Vessels*, finalist for the 2018 Kingsley Tufts Prize; *Nightingale*, winner of the 2020 Washington State Book Award for Poetry; and *West: A Translation*, which was longlisted for the 2023 National Book Award in Poetry and won the 2024 Kingsley Tufts Prize and the Mountains & Plains Bookseller's "Reading the West" Poetry Book Award. Her newest works of nonfiction include a book-length essay, *The Broken Country: On Trauma, a Crime, and the Continuing Legacy of Vietnam* and *Appropriate: A Provocation*. She guest edited *Best American Poetry 2020*. A pedagogy book has just been published: *Real Toads: Imaginary Gardens: On Reading and Writing Poetry Forensically* (W.W. Norton, 2024).

Gerard Robledo

THE LAST DAYS OF SUMMER

09-22-2025

During summer, mornings are cold.
  My body cracks—
a bundle of weak twigs across a boy's knee.

  Surprisingly, I'm forty-ish and not diabetic.
Still, when I stretch for my sandals and shirt,
  the worn cartilage and bone rubbing

together clears any doubts—splintering the daybreak
  like a rooster's call, a cock shouting behind my grandmother
at 5 a.m. Dios, she'd say, waking early just to watch

  the day careen past. My child needs
to rouse herself slowly
  with the kindred voices of other children

and adults with their hands up
  the asses of sock puppets
on PBS kids—that bent-over Kermit

  meme burned into my mind: his hand
hole rosebudding like pimento
  out of an olive, eliciting a desire

for a morning cigarette. But it's only Tuesday;
  there are still flat pancakes and fake bacon
to throw in the microwave while I lumber

  in the kitchen, preparing her lunch, missing my curlers
and vinyl slippers. My music just out of earshot:
  sometimes it's the ten years I lost, Passion Pit and Justice

sparking the electronic mornings; other times,
  it's the teen years I wish I were more
confident in, stuck in a loop—Ian Curtis and Iggy Pop

170

stepping out and spotting trains, with the living dead,
pale faced, black lips, and fishnets staggering into a Denny's
at 3 a.m. I *Choose Life*. Now, at forty, I need her

structure and sobriety to keep me accountable—I'm not.
 Sometimes she'll creep from behind: me, crisscross
applesauce at the coffee table. Her arms overtake

 as best a child can. Tiny fingers work around my throat
the other hand thrust in my armpit. I'm vulnerable
 to her tickles and questions. *Will you ever stop working?*

Failure to answer distresses her. My grandmother
 climbs out of her mouth, kitchen knife in hand,
following that question. She wants me to be everything:

 a good father and mother, nurturing like taught,
and masculine like I never saw; sew her skirt
 and knees together, then ignore the tampon

I'll eventually slide under the door.
 For her, I'll pretend I'm a dumb rock of a man
while I caress bruises and bake dinner.

 It's what my grandmother taught me while decrying
my mother's incapability. It's what I'll show my brothers
 men do with an iron and starch. Still, no answer.

When will I stop? My half-White daughter
 with strands of red, brown, and gold hair mixing
in the early blue-morning-half-light. I can't help

 but think of Molly Ringwald in *Pretty in Pink*
reprimanding her father for his lethargic mornings
 when she serves me a brunch of biscuits drizzled

with honey and a cocktail: her last Dreamsicle
 and Topo Chico over ice.
But she doesn't know her mom left us— me,

on a cracking cold morning. Near twelve, I miss her
more now—I realize the parenting part of being
a parent: schedules, recipes, and

implied domestication raises my profile
for women I don't know, but it doesn't
balance the guilt of freedom, my exploits:

Eat, Drink, & Fuck
stenciled in lavender on whitewashed shiplap,
not found at Pier 1, but maybe Family Dollar.

Gerard Robledo is a Mexican American poet from San Antonio and an Immigrant son. He holds an MFA in Creative Writing from the University of Texas at El Paso and teaches at Palo Alto College. His Spanish language poetry translations, poetry, and book reviews have appeared in *Voices de la Luna, The Texas Observer, Oyster River Pages, Solstice Magazine, Poetrybay, Vox Populi*, and others. He is the author of the poetry chapbook *My Mother, the Butcher* (Texas Review Press 2025), a Macondo Writers' Workshop Fellow, and a recipient of the 2020 Eduardo Corral Emerging Latinx Writers Mentorship.

Steve Scafidi

ON THE OCCASION OF AN ARGUMENT BESIDE THE RIVER WHERE I LIVE

10-09-2009

Someone says we are trapped in language, and so the sun drops overhead
    through stilly pines where the river explains nothing and far away now
    several men and women on the Yangtze look up from their nets and
    point to the sky.
Bright Chinese fish, like all my words struggle in the nets of a stranger.
But because there is no surprise nor delight in the hour of owl-call and
    locusts vibrating in the walnut trees, my friend despairs. All she hears
    are owls and locusts and though two grandfathers molder in the silk of
    their caskets and she loved them, the night is just the night.
And two men flying overhead from opposite directions embrace and
hover
    over the house, kicking their long spindly legs. Foolishness, I hear one
    say, foolishness.
Tonight the chatter of things is enormous and also the silence that allows
    such chatter—the empty space the tongue clicks through to make a
    word, the cataract between atoms a light thing might leap.
So, if there is nothing here, then the absence of the river makes the river
    possible.
And the slow stripping of all my clothes makes the heat of this July night
    a bearable delight and a secret joy, walking down the driveway, to the
    bank of the river, over the water-worked stones, and into the current.
Laura, I don't know what you are doing but I am swimming naked in the
    Shenandoah and the sun is in China, still rising over the Yangtze.
And there is nothing for you here if two men can't fly, skimming the
    surface of the water eating horseflies and laughing; and it is the truth,
    not my truth or some private certainty I tell you.
It is midnight and I sparkle like a trout.

Sometimes a long line is freeing. It gives you the space to think without the self consciousness and constant turning of shorter lines. Why not write a poem with long lines? The decisions we make about our lines—their length, their cadence, their tone—come from our sense of craft and something else, more curious. Sometimes the desire to write a poem is very specific in its dimensions. Sometimes I want a skeltonic jumping spider of a poem—or at least I sense some need or urgency that is best satisfied by the words taking that shape. Sometimes I want a redwood of a poem that begins under the earth and travels so far upward that I can't see the top of it. That would be the desire for something, perhaps, in a longer line. It is like my hunger for certain foods at certain times. Perhaps my body needs a carrot. Well, go get a carrot. We follow our instincts as writers and hope we have the craft to get there.

Steve Scafidi is a poet and cabinetmaker living in Summit Point, West Virginia.

Tim Seibles

TRYING FOR FIRE

10-05-2007

Right now, even if a muscular woman wanted
to teach me the power of her skin
I'd probably just stand here with my hands
jammed in my pockets. Tonight
I'm feeling weak as water, watching the wind
bandage the moon. That's how it is tonight:
sky like tar, thin gauzy clouds,
a couple lame stars. A car rips by—
the driver's cigarette pinwheels past
the dog I saw hit this afternoon.
One second he was trotting along
with his wet nose tasting the air,
next thing I know he's off the curb,
a car swerves and, bam, it's over. For an instant,
he didn't seem to understand he was dying—
he lifted his head as if he might still reach
the dark-green trash bags half-open
on the other side of the street.

I wish someone could tell me
how to live in the city. My friends
just shake their heads and shrug. I
can't go to church—I'm embarrassed by things
preachers say we should believe.
I would talk to my wife, but she's worried
about the house. Whenever she listens
she hears the shingles giving in
to the rain. If I read the paper
I start believing some stranger
has got my name in his pocket—
on a matchbook next to his knife.

When I was twelve I'd take out the trash—
the garage would open like some ogre's cave

175

while just above my head the Monday Night Movie
stepped out of the television, and my parents
leaned back in their chairs. I can still hear
my father's voice coming through the floor,
"Boy, make sure you don't make a mess down there."
I remember the red-brick caterpillar of row houses
on Belfield Avenue and, not much higher than the rooftops,
the moon, soft and pale as a nun's thigh.

I had a plan back then—my feet were made
for football: each toe had the heart
of a different animal, so I ran
ten ways at once. I knew I'd play pro,
and live with my best friend, and
when Vanessa let us pull up her sweater
those deep-brown balloony mounds made me believe
in a world where eventually you could touch
whatever you didn't understand.

If I was afraid of anything it was
my bedroom when my parents made me
turn out the light: that knocking noise
that kept coming from the walls,
the shadow shapes by the bookshelf,
the feeling that something was always there
just waiting for me to close my eyes.
But only sleep would get me, and I'd
wake up running for my bike, my life
jingling like a little bell on the breeze.
I understood so little that I
understood it all, and I still know
what it meant to be one of the boys
who had never kissed a girl.

I never did play pro football.
I never got to do my mad-horse,
mountain goat, happy-wolf dance
for the blaring fans in the Astro Dome.
I never snagged a one-hander over the middle
against Green Bay and stole my snaky way
down the sideline for the game-breaking six.

And now, the city is crouched like a mugger
behind me—right outside, in the alley behind my door,
a man stabbed this guy for his wallet, and sometimes
I see this four-year-old with his face all bruised,
his father holding his hand like a vise. When I
turn on the radio the music is just like the news.
So, what should I do—close my eyes and hope
whatever's out there will just let me sleep?
I won't sleep tonight. I'll stay near my TV
and watch the police get everybody.

Across the street a woman is letting
her phone ring. I see her in the kitchen
stirring something on the stove. Farther off
a small dog chips the quiet with his bark.
Above me the moon looks like a nickel
in a murky little creek. This
is the same moon that saw me twelve,
without a single bill to pay, zinging
soup can tops into the dark—I called them
flying saucers. This is the same
white light that touched dinosaurs, that
found the first people trying for fire.

It must have been very good, that moment
when wood smoke turned to flickering, when
they believed night was broken
once and for all—I wonder what almost-words
were spoken. I wonder how long
before that first flame went out.

Half the battle—if not more than half—is in finding language that seems both accurate (with regard to the subject) and inviting to a reader. If I didn't care about communicating I'd wouldn't write poems; I'd simply write in a diary or journal. A poem, in my eyes, is a public document of experience— meant to be shared. I think people read poetry to discover things about the world and about themselves. A poem is an invitation to think hard about the human condition, to recognize differences in experience and to see our own struggles in the lives/voices of others. If a poem is carelessly obscure it can't reveal anything worthwhile, and poetry is about revelation, not adding confusion to an already difficult world.

Tim Seibles is the author of several collections of poetry including *Hurdy-Gurdy*, *Hammerlock*, *Buffalo Head Solos*, *One Turn Around The Sun*, and *Fast Animal*, which was a finalist for the 2012 National Book Award and winner of the Theodore Roethke Memorial Poetry Prize. His New & Selected collection, *Voodoo Libretto* was released in 2021. His next book, *With No Hat*, will be published in 2026.

Said Shaiye

A FELA KUTI STORY

10-06-2025

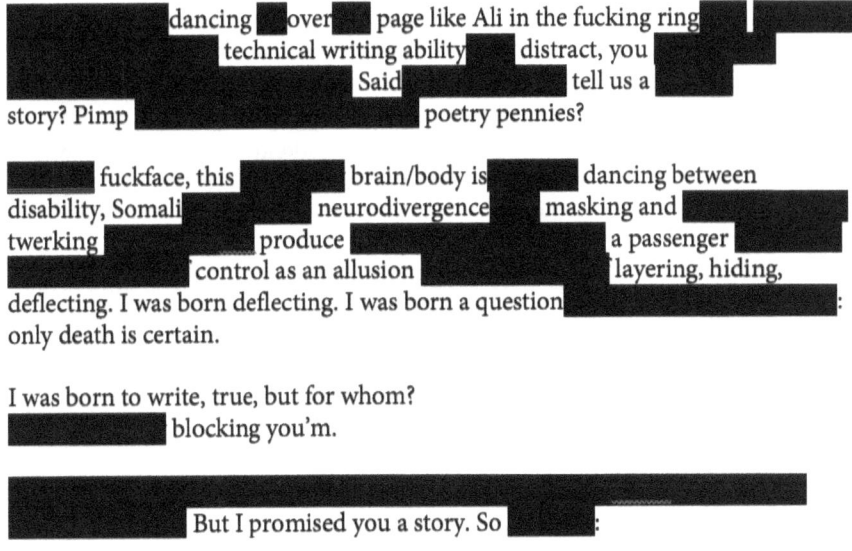

dancing ▮ over ▮ page like Ali in the fucking ring
technical writing ability▮ distract, you
Said ▮ tell us a
story? Pimp ▮ poetry pennies?

▮ fuckface, this ▮ brain/body is ▮ dancing between
disability, Somali ▮ neurodivergence ▮ masking and
twerking ▮ produce ▮ a passenger
▮ control as an allusion ▮ layering, hiding,
deflecting. I was born deflecting. I was born a question ▮:
only death is certain.

I was born to write, true, but for whom?
▮ blocking you'm.

▮ But I promised you a story. So ▮:

Fela Kuti said: "I want to tell you a story." He never
tells you the story.

Simply states: "put your legs & arms together....
Open & Close... Throw your legs & arms away."

He teaches you how to dance as you wait for a story
which never unfolds.

As if the dance can force you to feel a story. When
words fail, dance, feel.
Open. Story. Close.

When a honeybee discovers fresh pollen, it returns to
the hive & says "Fela Kuti."

The bee begins to dance thereafter. Story, Open.
The Hive watches, learns, patient. Story, Closed.

The dance is not a dance but a map of steps. A language hidden in rhythm. A map to glory, to pollen, to the meaning of feeling. A Fela Kuti feeling which words, countries, years cannot teach or convey. A story, a hope. Close

Now here we stand before you like the first of some brand-new fucking species, quoting Kuti like Proost (not Proust), stealing lines from Alfie Solomons, words lurching over you like a goliath of unspeakable dimensions, claiming to tell you a story. I, we, just want you to feel what it's like to be born into a war. How surviving is sometimes a worse fate than death. No. Story. Close. Legs. Arms. Away.

Perhaps I'm not the right man to tell this story; too sensitive. Perhaps I care more about myself than your entertainment. Perhaps I just don't care. In the psych ward, we used to say: I don't care about being alive, why would I care about you?

Open.
Story.
Fela.
Bee.
Kuti.
Dance.
Close.

I wish I could tell you this story, could open myself, but the gates of trauma remain closed. A dam, a Sisyphean boulder, the levees just before Katrina made landfall. Sometimes we erect walls around ourselves hoping to keep the world at bay, or to keep the pain within. Sometimes we care so much about others that we can't let that pain out. As if the pain is Katrina, or the heart is a levee, or the story is taking shelter in a football stadium, praying this isn't the last place we see before eternal destiny.

I want to tell you a story.

It has no happy endings, no known beginning. It is a love story which grew by the shadow under which nothing can grow.

It is not supposed to be possible. A myth, like

180

meteor goldfish. And yet, here it is, on a subreddit, discovered by a fish tank cleaner.

Yet here it stands, here I stand, open, close (to you), having grown in a place that speaks a tongue which punctuates every phrase with death. We escaped the war, the grave awaits, stack that bread, accrue, hope for a final payoff in the world beyond.

Maalik Sidibey taught me how to steal people's genie souls inside his Bamako studio. This is a metaphor or obfuscation.

Perhaps the real issue is that a story construct cannot hold the meaning of life *or*: what it means to think you are alive.

Perhaps this sentence is the last thought you will have post-mortem.

The lingering electrochemical signals sent from brain to body which cause limb twitches despite obvious death written on body, etched in face, to those who boldly face: falsehoods, steps retraced, pockets full of posy regrets, ringworm around Rosemary's head, wreaths, wraiths, weight... Haight, Berries of Ash, Tinsel Tonsils, Cabbage Patch, Asinine like expecting introspection from Travis Scott lines.

A coroner coughs begonias. A poet welcomes you home. Look, son, this is all we own:
> *the land, but only if it hasn't*
> *by white men been stole.*

We flyover this stolen land. The thieves our pilots, preaching Stonewall Jackson, confederate captains, mumbling unsure quips like "*just want to get their history right.*" Start by giving that land back. Pay back that life-debt. But you don't want that.

You stole this place, washed its history away with the blood of your victims, now flex email signatures with "*living on stolen land of such & such tribe.*" Your victims' bodies hang from clothes wire like so much lost linen; skeletons littering swampland like strange fruit scarecrows.

Forever Free Palestine.

I wrote this poem in Miami. I went there for my yearly "winter depression getaway from Minneapolis to somewhere warm," but I started it at a visual art library in Minneapolis. I would go there, get high on matcha/coffee & flip through random visual art books. One of them was by Malick Sidibé, a Malian photographer whose work I immediately fell in love with. The Fela Kuti thing is from a song that has always stayed with me—and how he never actually tells you the story, but teaches you how to dance. So we dance when we mean to write, cry when we mean to laugh. This is a poet's life, an immigrant life, a neurodivergent and disabled life.

I am allergic to poetic form and the boxes they force us into. My style has always dwelled between prose and poetry, with a surrealist tint, and a need for freedom. I come from an oral poetry tradition and started my career as a spoken word artist. The somali language didn't even have a written alphabet until the 70s. English isn't my first language, so my subject/verb order is still Somali. All of this makes me appear to be a poet, yet I struggle to obey line breaks, forms, stanzas, order. I crave coffee and chaos. I don't know how the hell I've tricked myself into believing I'm a writer. But there is no other way I can exist in this world.

Said Shaiye is an Autistic + ADHD (AuHD) Somali writer and photographer in Minneapolis. He is represented by Mariah Stovall at Trellis Literary Management. He is a 2024 MacDowell Colony Fellow as well as a 2024 AWP Panelist on "Autistic Writers On the Inaccessibility of Professional Writing Spaces," and "The Anti-Ableist Writing Workshop." He was nominated for a 2024 Pushcart Prize by Indiana Review for his essay "Sneak a Uzi on the Island in My Army Jacket Lining." His debut book, *Are You Borg Now?* was a 2022 Minnesota Book Award finalist in Creative Nonfiction and Memoir. He has published poetry and prose in *Indiana Review*, *The Texas Review*, *Obsidian*, *Brittle Paper*, *Pithead Chapel*, *580 Split*, *Entropy*, *Diagram*, and elsewhere.

Enid Shomer

DRIVING THROUGH THE ANIMAL

11-17-2016

Through my window, the buzz of a distant combine
cutting a swath through the far pasture of rye,
small animals caught in its wheeling blades—
rabbits shived to wet ribbons, field mice
reduced to minims of bloody fur as the field
flattens into the lush avenues of our hungers.

At drivers' school last fall I learned it's a fatal
mistake to spare the deer, possum or pet
in the road. Drive through the animal, the officer
said. Since flesh gives, collision—even
with a steer—is safer than a wild swerve
into oncoming traffic, culvert, or tree.

I know how it happens: past midnight near Cedar Key,
the road cinching up on its yellow thread.
Star-bright eyes cluster like low constellations.
I drive through the herd, the car my armor,
telling myself they're only a thicket of bone
and blood. Like faint quarter moons, hooves rise

in my headlights, a body slams—brief trophy—
on the grille. Deer often die of fright
before they die of their wounds. But mine casts
in the road for hours, its tongue spilled, flies
working the open spots, vultures sifting
down from trees. The truth is I'd never drive

straight through. Whatever it is that leaps
in my chest would become what leapt in the road,
and I'd turn away. Try as I might that night in school
to steer my dummy wheel into films of deer
and dogs dashing headlong or popping up
as placards, I couldn't let their blood
become my wine.

Enid Shomer is the author of five poetry collections, two short story collections and a novel. Her poems have appeared in literary journals and magazines including *The Atlantic Monthly, Poetry, Paris Review, The New Criterion, Parnassus, Kenyon Review, Tikkun*, and in anthologies including *The Best American Poetry.* Her new collection, *Riptide: New and Selected Poems* is forthcoming in June 2026.

ire'ne lara silva

IN MY HEART

08-22-2023

in my heart no circus
in my heart no cages
in my heart no stampedes
in my heart no whirlpools
in my heart no quicksand
in my heart no raging fires
in my heart no guilt
in my heart no shame
in my heart no chaos
in my heart no bitterness
in my heart nothing left unsaid

in my heart tawny fields of tall grass
in my heart drifting clouds
in my heart flowering vines
in my heart mesquites and huizaches
in my heart sycamores and cedars
in my heart every small and humble green
in my heart blooming ocotillos and crowns of thorns
in my heart the peaceful lapping of the wide river
in my heart the light of his eyes that will never leave me
in my heart a thousand thousand conversations
in my heart the hand i held even after it went cold

my friend said, you see, hardly anyone knows what peaceful grief looks like

---

We're quick to dismiss lists as first sight—thinking that stories can only come in certain forms, thinking that lists are easy to dismiss, thinking that repetition is a mask for a lack of depth. Instead, we find that list poems build like a wave, the tension winding higher and higher, until finally, they crash into us with devastating effect.

ire'ne lara silva, 2023 Texas Poet Laureate, is the author of five poetry collections, *furia*, *Blood Sugar Canto*, *CUICACALLI/House of Song*, *firstPoems*, and *the eaters of flowers*, two chapbooks, *Enduring Azucares* and *Hibiscus Tacos*, a comic book, *Vendaval*, and a short story collection, *flesh to bone*, which won the Premio Aztlán. ire'ne is the recipient of the 2021 Texas Institute of Letters Shrake Award for Best Short Nonfiction, a 2021 Tasajillo Writers Grant, a 2017 NALAC fund for the Arts Grant, the final Alfredo Cisneros del Moral Award, and was the fiction finalist for AROHO's 2013 Gift of freedom Award. ire'ne is currently a Writer at Large for *Texas Highways Magazine*. Her second short story collection, *the light of your body*, was published by Arte Publico Press in 2025.

Leah Silvieus

MATTHEW 19:14

02-24-2024

after Jericho Brown
for the camp girls

Heaven belongs to such as these
    Your apostle taught us,

so Lord, let me not forget:
    those six girlhood summers down

that two-lane highway, left—past
    the seven-foot plastic Hereford bull

at Clearwater Junction; sleeping
    in cast-off army tents

where forty-miles-away
    might've been a different country, those

faraway towns' names exotic:
    Philipsburg, Frenchtown,

Wisdom, Choteau—
    bless those mouths red

with Fla-Vor-Ice, singing
    rise and shine and give God the glory,

glory. As we waited for the mess tent dinner bell
    the counselors decreed,

the last shall be first
    and the first shall be last

and we all turned 'round in line
　　　because we believed

that one day it'd be true.
　　　Lord forget us not in our hour

of need— those who dug Dixie cups
　　　from trash bins to tear into visions

of the Blessed Virgin, who stole change from Right to Life
　　　coin banks to buy Ring Pops for our little sisters.

Bless us, Lord, we dirt-road orphans, grown now
　　　and miles from the closest home—

girls once named for virtues
　　　our mothers hoped we'd hold true:

Faith, Joy, and daughter after daughter
　　　　　　　called Mercy.

Leah Silvieus was born in South Korea and adopted to the U.S. at three-months old. She grew up in small towns in Montana's Bitterroot Valley and western Colorado. She is the author of *Anemochory* (Hyacinth Girl Press), *Season of Dares* (Bull City Press), *Arabilis* (Sundress Publications) and co-editor with Lee Herrick of the poetry anthology, *The World I Leave You: Asian American Poets on Faith and Spirit* (Orison Books). She is a recipient of awards and fellowships from Kundiman, The Academy of American Poets, and Fulbright and serves as a mentor on The Brooklyn Poets Bridge. A 2019-2020 National Book Critics Circle Emerging Fellow, Leah serves as a senior books editor at *Hyphen* magazine and an associate editor at *Marginalia Review of Books*. Her reviews and criticism have appeared in the *Harvard Review Online*, *The Believer*, and elsewhere.

ML Smoker

TATOGANA

03-17-2021

Yes, this year has been hard on all of us. The
antelope have taken to crossing the lake, maybe
attempting an instinctual, yet impossible move to
warmer climates. Just last week the ice gave way and
more than eighty were lost to the lake's cold water, limbs
and hooves torn from the fight to break free. Those who
had been spared stood looking on in both misery and
curiosity. When the rescue team and boats arrived, they
rushed to pull as many as possible to safety. Then in so
short a time the only work left was loading heavy
carcasses and hauling them to land. Quickly, as it does
this time of year, evening came and the crews moved
toward their vehicles, the bloated antelope piled in the
beds of their pickups. Only when the engines started did
the animals left on the lake's dark shore stir, their gaunt
faces lingering and unafraid in the red glow of taillights
moving back toward town.

A member of the Sioux and Assiniboine tribes, poet M.L. Smoker earned a BA
at Pepperdine University and an MFA at the University of Montana, where she
received the Richard Hugo Memorial Scholarship. Smoker also studied at UCLA,
where she received the Arianna and Hannah Yellow Thunder Scholarship, and the
University of Colorado, where she was a Battrick Fellow. Smoker is the author of
the poetry collection *Another Attempt at Rescue* (2005). With Melissa Kwasny, she
co-edited *I Go to the Ruined Place: Contemporary Poems in Defense of Global Human
Rights* (2009). Smoker lives in Helena, Montana, where she works in the Indian
Education Division of the Office of Public Instruction.

Angela Narciso Torres

THINGS TO TELL MY SON ABOUT THE MOON

08-26-2019

She seemed so close those October nights
on the bentwood rocker—her bright disc
rising at the wheel-shaped window

like the first face that greeted
your pale crescent of scalp before
its triumphant push into light. Then

I came to know the near perfect roundness
of your head, silver-downed, nestled
against my breast, taut with milk. Skin

to skin we watched the night pour out
from a ladle, tilted to spill the slow
spooling hours. In the silken silence

of a moth's cocoon, I listened for
the sound of your swallows, followed
the motions of your starfish hand, patting,

pulling loose a strand of my hair.
Somewhere I learned which cry meant
you had enough, or wanted more.

From spring to harvest moon I watched
the shadows move across your face,
explored new regions with borrowed light.

Born in Brooklyn and raised in Manila, Angela Narciso Torres has authored three poetry collections, most recently *What Happens Is Neither* (four Way Books). A graduate of Warren Wilson MFA Program and Harvard Graduate School of Education, she has received fellowships from Bread Loaf Writers' Conference and Ragdale foundation. Recent work appears in *32 Poems*, *Prairie Schooner*, and *Alaska Quarterly Review*. She lives in San Diego and serves as reviews editor for *RHINO Poetry*.

Brian Turner

CURFEW

05-13-2007

The wrong is not in the religion;
The wrong is in us.
—Saier T.

At dusk, bats fly out by the hundreds.
Water snakes glide in the ponding basins
behind the rubbled palaces. The mosques
call their faithful in, welcoming
the moonlight as prayer.

Today, policemen sunbathed on traffic islands
and children helped their mothers
string clothes to the line, a slight breeze
filling them with heat.

There were no bombs, no panic in the streets.
Sgt. Gutierrez didn't comfort an injured man
who cupped pieces of his friend's brain
in his hands; instead, today,
white birds rose from the Tigris.

Brian Turner is the author of five collections of poetry, most recently: *The Wild Delight of Wild Things* (2023), *The Goodbye World Poem* (2023), and *The Dead Peasant's Handbook* (2023). His other collections include *Here, Bullet* to *Phantom Noise*, and the memoir *My Life as a Foreign Country*. He is the editor of *The Kiss* and co-editor of *The Strangest of Theatres* anthologies. A musician, he has also written and recorded several albums with The Interplanetary Acoustic Team, including *I I I I (Me Smiling)* and The Retro Legion's *American Undertow*. His poems and essays have been published in *The New York Times*, *The Guardian*, *National Geographic*, *Harper's*, among other fine journals, and he was featured in the documentary film *Operation Homecoming: Writing the Wartime Experience*, which was nominated for an Academy Award. A Guggenheim Fellow, he has received a USA Hillcrest Fellowship in Literature, the Amy Lowell Traveling Fellowship, the Poets' Prize, and a Fellowship from the Lannan Foundation. He lives in Orlando, Florida, with his dog, Dene, the world's sweetest golden retriever.

Connie Voisine

THE EARLY DAYS OF AVIATION

10-01-2011

St. Exupery stayed in the hotel between flights
for the postal service. Then, they navigated by landmarks—
a farmhouse, a body of water—and,
when those were made invisible, a compass,
and flashlight. No wonder he imagined
a prince on a tiny planet
as he hurled himself against the constellations.
The world was a dark scroll unrolling beneath
and the plane could become a vehicle you'd use
the way a gnat uses its wings, with a three-dimensional
fluidity and the world might feel to you
the way water must feel to a dolphin.
It was too cold in that hotel, wind
snaked through the cracked-framed windows
and faded drapes. I was easily distracted—too cold

for too long. I could tell you this was the year that I too
flew through a darkness, but at the time
I only felt ugly, inarticulate. I'd take a hot bath
every other night for 5 extra francs. So hot
I barely breathed for a half-hour
after emerging, my heart still beating hard and fast.
I'd go directly to bed and sleep 10 hours. Too cold
and I wanted the day to pass so I could
start over. In the papers, an 80 year old
named Papon was being tried as a collaborator
for the Nazis. During the trial,
his frail wife died, a result of stress. Papon explained
that he took the papers handed to him by Germans,
signed them, and sent the papers on. This is what
kept him alive, he said, signing these papers
which sent hundreds of French Jews to the gas chambers.
The young Papon was dapper in the wartime
photos, his wife well-shod and I wondered at how

what doesn't happen at its neglected moment
flares up, virulent, more so from regret.
How we are all accountable and how it never stops.
Sometimes, I eavesdropped on the nasal

American couple next door—animated in the hallway,
a key in a lock, and I held my breath. Him, with his athletic
stomach and sideburns talking much and more
than she. They wore the banal uniform of American travelers,
as if they might be forced to tear through a jungle
or conquer a mountain, but nighttime
she wore a rich leather jacket with scalloped details
on the pockets and cuffs. Lying in my creaking,
deep-slung bed, lonely, I imagined speaking
before them. We'd make plans and their casual natures
were very attractive, made me feel at ease. I imagined
sitting at dinner with them—why? In my vision
I was flushed, internal, explaining what it is
to be a writer. That one is constantly revealing oneself.
That, as a result, a writer always needs love
but never can remember being loved enough. I'd wrestle

the pillows and debate turning on the light
to read my textbook about French cathedrals, muttering,
what do I think they can give me?
I would sometimes try to imagine what it would be
to play in the sky.
The medieval builders of cathedrals abandoned
barbaric forms, wrote M. Guy Duby—the vegetal motifs,
the repetition of abstract designs. They moved towards
grander, more elaborate forms
of worship—gold and splendor, biblical
tales reproduced in whole, hundreds
of angels carved in stone as if making it look
human could dissolve the terror
of mystery. I wondered at barbarism—the combination
of the real, minor vine and leaf with the fathomless,
solid expression of a circle inside a square.
I looked around my hotel room at the strewn
clothing, the chipped sink that leaned from the wall, the crack

in the plaster that looked like a man leaping
over the dresser. I understood that the only thing I wanted
from this world was that it need me. And it
did not—a woman waiting in her bed
because there was nowhere she would go. And weren't those
the fearless, early days of aviation—a plane,
the tiny arrow shooting towards an oblivion of sky, wind,
the spree of flight, the eventual
crumpled metal in a farmer's field?

Connie Voisine is the author, most recently of *The Bower* (2019) and the chapbook of poems, *And God Created Women*. A previous book, *Rare High Meadow of Which I Might Dream*, was a finalist for the *Los Angeles Times* Book Award. Her first book, *Cathedral of the North*, won the Associated Writing Program's Award in Poetry. She has poems published in *The New Yorker*, *The Georgia Review*, *Ploughshares*, *Poetry Magazine*, *Black Warrior Review*, *The Threepenny Review*, and elsewhere. Educated at Yale University, University of California at Irvine, and University of Utah, Voisine was a Fulbright Fellow to Queen's University in Belfast, Northern Ireland.

Mark Wagenaar

CHIROPRACTIC (BOOTBLACKS & LIGHT BULBS)

04-28-2014

for Chelsea Marie Henderson

Not the massage you were expecting,
but one that parts the many waters
of your back muscles-*latissismus dorsi,*
trapezius, the ones that sound so much
like stars, *rhomboideus minor, iliocostalis-*
until the vertebrae, living stones, sing,
right down to the sacrum-named
the 'sacred bone' by the Greeks
because the soul resides there-down
to the coccyx, formed by vestigial
vertebrae & named for the cuckoo's
bill it resembles, & as two hands
memorize each angle until even
the fossae-the small depressions
only the wind knows about-hum
like wineglasses, you sink into a sleep
like waking, a dream like forgetting,
& the answer to the last crossword clue—
what do bootblacks & lightbulbs do—hovers
like a crow over withered fields, unknowable,
& you try to remember the body's
fourteen stations-or was that something
else entirely-is there one for clavicle,
for what follows joy, one for what sparks
grief, were desire & laughter two halves
of one station, because it feels like they should be,
& where on the list were the ankles' sharp
spurs, or hands holding water, tongue
tasting lemongrass, liver remembering
malbec, none of them the answer that is always
just out of reach, just beyond the misdirection
& sleight-of-hand memory plays, & no, it wasn't Fu

195

Manchu who wrote *dry creek bed glimpsed*
by lightning, that's ridiculous, it was oh
the look on his face when he saw you
by morning light for the first time, it was something
like a blessing for they who thirst,
something like grace-mercy for the undeserving,
rain where there are no clouds-it was an answer,
in the synapses' electric blue voids, an answer
somewhere in the fault lines of the body, *shine*.

To offer up someone's discovery of the body as a place of both transcendence and memory—those are very different things, of course, and I wondered what transcendence looked like, if we can call something transcendence if it resembles something we've known all along-some valence we reach when memory, eros, and the sacred collide. I wasn't as interested in the idea of enlightenment reached through meditation, or long suffering, or sustained prayer, but rather a more ordinary kind-an everyday enlightenment, a blue-collar transcendence. And it became more and more apparent that the process itself, the road to getting there, was extremely important to the poem-especially because the final bit of knowledge realized is just an answer/pun to a crossword puzzle, if the answer doesn't evoke an associational barrage of everything else that shines, which is what I was hoping for-a lingering post-poem blaze of the world's ten thousand things (good to be ambitious about one's own work, I guess). So the single sentence is at once an enactment of this stream of thought as well as a form that allows the reader to (hopefully) better follow this stream.

This poem is partially a "found" poem. My roommate at the time, Aja, had left her crossword beside a lamp, and I came back from teaching one morning to find that clue-and the riddle became the underlying, and perhaps most important, structure within the poem. Of course, if you're an avid puzzler, you might know the answer right away-a bit of a risk I decided I would take.

Mark Wagenaar is a father of three, and husband to poet Chelsea Wagenaar. He's the author of three prize-winning volumes of poetry, and his poetry and fiction appear widely. He works as a realtor and broker in Raleigh.

Michael Walsh

THE GHOST STORY THEY TELL ABOUT YOU

10-13-2025

Dear Father, did you know the summer you spent in the hospital
in St. Peter for the dangerous and mentally ill,

I was in town too? I was falling in love with a boy
at summer camp, thinking about you in a straitjacket,

strapped down for shock therapy, drugged up
and playing cards with other lunatics, not that I knew

anything about your diagnosis or days. I only knew I blew
our best chance to meet. You couldn't leave.

I could've brought my secret boyfriend, a deck of cards,
dealt a game of hearts for three. I could've let you win.

Would you have told me what it felt like to nail your house
shut, window and door, your wife and daughter

asleep inside, how quiet you kept your hammer?
And after you started the fire, how you stuck around

to watch the show or split to smoke or pop something
in celebration? I would've listened because I want

to know who you were really burning, how
happy or terrible you felt when your wife wrenched

open a window, the two of them scared out of their minds.
I want to know what black magic charms you used

on my mother, then my aunt, while you called
our house saying I know where you live, bitch,

and I'm gonna getcha. For years I mouthed your threat
like the alphabet, those secondhand words.

197

How many teenage girlfriends did you get pregnant
in your forty-eight years, how many other kids still out there?

And why did women keep falling for you? There are no answers
about the night you and your brother, playing with a gun,

shot and killed your little sister. Did you pull
the trigger? Did you blame him? My mother swears it; my aunt

defends you. I want to know if that lie could've forced you
to your feet during the funeral after his suicide to cry out

You don't know shit about pain to the priest. The day you chased
your mother with a knife out of her house, then your father

down the alley with a gun shooting wildly, I knew
I'd never know the truth about you. I was thirteen,

worried I might start hearing gravestones speak,
wake up one morning covered in my family's blood.

Michael Walsh is the author of *The Dirt Riddles*, which received the Miller Williams Prize and the Thom Gunn Award for Gay Poetry, as well as *Creep Love*, a 2022 finalist for the Lambda Literary Award in Gay Poetry. Most recently Autumn House Press published *Queer Nature*, the first ecoqueer American poetry anthology and a 2023 finalist for the Lambda Literary Award in Anthologies. Living in the Driftless region of southwest Wisconsin, Michael is developing Queer Nature teachings and workshops.

Sarah Rebecca Warren

CHIMAYÓ MILAGROS

03-18-2019

In the room of miracle dirt, women weep,
        rock back and forth over a decades old pit.
        One bends down to scoop cinnamon brown
granules, and she eats. She sobs, chews the grit.

        Is it miracles or the heroin, or adobe walls
against turquoise sky that draws the faithful
to this altar of hope, to find solace in a pinch
        of powder? That theater of knee-bent repentance—

devotion to something just out of reach.
        The voice of a life of crucifixions hums outside.
        Perhaps it's the one who sprouted from dry soil.
I practice the saints, sign of the cross, and search

        for milagros through sacred hearts and our ladies.
The man outside sings me to him, breathes deep.
He feeds me pistachios, fresh ground chili.
        He thinks in a past life we were saints,

we were born of something more than fire—
        pero éste no es el poema que deseo escribir.
        There is no miracle here, but blood shot eyes,
wild-running children and graffiti splashed

        on sacred walls. Here is where I learn that the heart
is not practical; that the man with an opiate twitch
will always stand at the foot of a curio shop just across
        from where pilgrims pray and consume the earth.

Sarah Rebecca Warren, Ph.D. is a writer, educator, and musician who lives in Denver, Colorado. Her writing has appeared in *Oklahoma Today, Gravel, Luna Luna,* and *World Literature Today,* among other magazines and journals. Her poems "Anatomy of an Eating Disorder" and "Chimayó Milagros" won first place in the *Arcturus* Fall 2017 Poetry Contest, adjudicated by Ruben Quesada. Sarah's chapbook, *Price of Admission,* appears in *Floodgate Poetry Series Volume 5* (Upper Rubber Boot Books, March 2019).

L. Lamar Wilson

TIMES LIKE THESE: MARIANNA, FLORIDA

11-18-2014

One woe is past; &, behold, there come two woes more hereafter.
—Revelation 9:12

In one field, corn husks, muscadine vines & a sugar cane graveyard furrow acres aching for the devil to beat his wife. In another, a skein of maggots & mayflies, their musk thick & resolute, jockey for the cow's afterbirth. Down Old U.S. Road apiece, weevils wheeze & chafed bales of hay settle for the wind's sneezes. *Wait for a sign*, the couple says & set their table with damask, fresh-pressed for a feast of sardines & cornbread. Train their child in the way he should babble. From dusk till dusk, they lull the boy with tales of a faraway sea, buckets of oysters to shuck. *OurFatherwhichartinheavenhallowedbethynamethykingdom comethywillbedoneonearthasitisinheaven*. Still no rain. From dusk till dusk, they till dust. Then they reach for the locks of hair & black-eyed peas, stowed away for times like these.

L. Lamar Wilson (he/we) is the author of *Sacrilegion* (Carolina Wren Press, 2013), a Thom Gunn finalist, and associate producer of *The Changing Same* (PBS/POV, 2019). He's published widely, including in *Callaloo*, *The Nation*, *This Is the Honey* (Hatchette, 2024), *Bigger than Bravery* (Lookout Books, 2022), the Academy of American Poets' *Poem-a-Day*, *New York Times*, *Oxford American*, and *Poetry*. Wilson, an Affrilachian Poet, has received fellowships from the Cave Canem, Civitella Ranieri, Hurston-Wright, and Ragdale foundations. He teaches creative writing, African American poetics, and film and gender studies at Florida State University and Mississippi University for Women.

Jennifer Yáñez-Alaniz

PATRON SAINT OF MOIST THINGS

10-25-2023

*I must be a mermaid, … I have no fear of depth and
great fear of shallow living.*
—Anaïs Nin

When I pray for love, I imagine our youth
and Anaïs Nin—

her wet verses underneath our tongues,
her sex an unguent between our bodies.

My tempered knees
tender & buckling at your waist, seeking salve
and chrism.

In my surrender,
In my memory, you untie the blue ribbon
from around my thigh, your teeth releasing the knot.
My openness tastes of fig and tamarind,
glistened cadence on the tongue.

I don't know you without the warm sun,
without summer's rain arced above our bodies,
without the milk-like sky anointing us with grace.

I long for your witness to my sanctity.
I long for your witness to my breasts,
swollen like a sea of darkness.

Jennifer Yáñez-Alaniz | Chicana Tú sìs Ndé scholar and poet is a dedicated community organizer and PhD fellow in the Culture, Literacy, and Language Program at the University of Texas at San Antonio and Graduate Certificate holder of Mexican American Studies. With over 15 years of experience as an educator, Jen currently works with preclinical teachers seeking bilingual/dual language and English as a second language certification. Her work is driven by a passion for challenging systemic inequalities and advocating for cultural preservation through the application of decolonial epistemologies, fostering transformative dialogues and inclusive educational practices. Her current research interests include land as pedagogy and translingualism as spatial theory both framed within a decolonial praxis.

Matthew Yeager

A BIG BALL OF FOIL IN A SMALL NY APARTMENT

02-02-2017

It will flame out....
—Hopkins

It began with a single sheet, leftover from his lunch.
His unthinking palm had reached out to it, slapped down
on the center of it, and begun gathering and compacting
until soon he had a small firm ball in his fist.
He squeezed the ball tightly, as tightly as he could.
Now the ball was, if not as firm as possible,
at least as firm as he could easily make it,
and he took from this the small satisfaction it offered.
It felt good. In fact, as his fingers opened out
into their individual selves again, and he saw the ball
resting in his slightly red, dented palm, as in a nest,
it occurred to him that there were many good things
to be felt about this ball: its crinkled surface
would keep it from rolling off at the slightest tilt;
it wouldn't come undone on it own as balled-up paper can;
and that it was all crumpled foil, 100% through
seemed to contain a kind of meaning,
(though truly what it was he wasn't sure)....
It was then that he had an idea. Like light on water
it danced across his thinking, absorbing his attention.
He would add to this ball, add to it until it was huge!
He wouldn't throw it out as he had so many others.
And how many had he thrown out? The unknowable number
(exaggerated for effect) jostled him all over, like nerves,
for you see, he had already begun to imagine the ball quite large,
and the thought that the foil in his little ball
might have existed as a nearly flat sheet on the surface
of an already enormous ball boggled him.
(But he knew it wasn't good to think like that,
and he snapped quickly to, nodding and determined.)
He would grow the ball from this point forward.

Foil was everywhere. It wouldn't be hard.
So from that day on as he walked the streets,
although he let his thoughts drift as they wished,
(seeing, for instance, the sun seep free from behind a cloud
he'd think, in the brief spell before it disappeared behind another,
of hundreds of suddenly pleased sunbathers in rows on a beach;
he'd think of sweaty red-faced men carrying heavy wooden crates)
he kept his sights always alive to the prospect
of foil's particular glint. When he'd see a stranded sheet
in a corner garbage can or on a restaurant table,
he'd glance sharply about, to see if anyone was watching him,
slyly pocket it, then shuffle off at a quickened pace.
Early on, it bothered him, and he'd have to reassure himself:
"No one is looking; no one cares; this city is full
of stranger things than a man collecting foil."
Over time, he began to believe this truth, or rather,
the shame he couldn't help but feel was overcome.
For there was nothing much better than walking about,
as twilight approached, with a good take bulging his pockets.
It was a feeling not unlike knowing a wonderful secret,
or being, perhaps, a bottle with a message in it.
However, at such bright excited times,
much like an island surfacing in a drought-sucked stream,
the ball as he wished it could be, huge and shining
and exactly round, would give rise in his mind.
It was awesome and beautiful, but not a good thing,
and he tried to keep it from happening, to hide it away,
like that heart under the floorboards in the Poe story
that had so terrified him as a child. For his own ball
when he'd return home, became so inadequate then,
so silly and lopsided and small. Emptying his pockets,
smoothing the foil with a rolling pin (his system),
he'd murmur sound, sobering sayings to himself like:
"nothing turns out the way you thought it would,"
and "it'll take years." But time was one thing he had,
and his progress, albeit slow (as each added scrap was a smaller
and smaller piece of the growing whole) was steady.
As the months went by, the ball grew. It grew and grew.
It grew until it had to be moved from the oven,
where he'd kept it to save space, into the open, onto the floor.
It grew till it couldn't fit through the window or the door.

It grew until furniture had to be moved, first
to new places in his apartment, then out onto the street.
It was then he knew the ball was there to stay....
But though he'd been the one that had wanted the ball,
though he'd been the one that had built the ball,
often he felt ambivalently, and this ambivalence grew too.
Why was he doing what he was?
Why was he filling his apartment, his mind, with foil?
It was not something he preferred to wonder about,
and he tried hard to keep the wondering out, to ignore it
as one might a dog that's scratching at a door....
But ridiculous as he acknowledged the ball to be,
if you were to have caught him at the right moment,
you would have seen how he loved it.
Certain nights, after he'd measured it in all directions
(by setting up a spotlight and measuring the shadows)
then peeled and patched it to preserve its roundness,
(the ball's defining, so most important quality)
he'd step away (as away as he still could),
and those narrowed-up, fault-inventing eyes of his
would soften into something like appreciation.
Spot-lit like that, the ball gave back a cool, fragile light
much as he heard the earth did when seen by astronauts,
and he'd feel suddenly lucky to be where he was,
standing in such strange and silvery shine. Coming to,
he'd often find an inch of ash on his cigarette....
So it was kind of sad then, that his ball should end,
should stop growing, even though all along
it'd been what he'd been working towards.
Would he still see a city speckled with foil?
Or would what once was treasure dull
to trash again? There was no way to predict.
The night he was done, the night the ball
nudged up against his ceiling and his walls
(a coincidence so long foreseen it had lost its luster)
he pressed his teeth deep into its surface,
as a kind of unreadable signature,
leaned his confused body against it, closed his eyes,
and, listening to the cars pass, wept a little bit.

Matthew Yeager's poems have appeared in *American Poetry Review*, Academy of American Poets *Poem-a-Day*, *Best American Poetry 2005, 2010, 2024* and elsewhere. "A Big Ball of foil in a Small NY Apartment," his micro-budget short film, was an official selection at eleven film festivals in 2009-2010, picking up three awards. Other distinctions include the Barthelme Prize in short prose, multiple fellowships to MacDowell and Yaddo, and inclusion in Oprah Magazine's "50 Beautiful Love Poems Begging to be Shared." The co-curator of the KGB Monday Night Poetry Series from 2011 - 2021, Yeager's first book, *Like That*, received a starred review from *Publisher's Weekly*. He is married to the poet Chelsea Whitton and currently teaches at the University of Cincinnati and the Art Academy of Cincinnati.

Jake Adam York

DARKLY

02-02-2017

for Dave Smith

The moss never falls.
However gray,

it hangs like shirts
left to weather and rag

over the road
and the dead-end rail

and in all the branches
from there to the shore

and then as far upriver
as you can see.

Here it's only open water,
empty sky,

two ends of road no one uses,
landfill on one side, thicket

on the other,
the story of a bridge between.

Below, the water's huddled,
cold and silver.

It won't show a thing.
So I look for that place in the air

where they held a gun
on Willie Edwards

and told him he could jump.
How you'd ask me-

Why's so simple
it won't tell a thing-

how'd they get there,
Edwards in their hands,

along the roads so many others took
to church or to the movies

or home
along the same white lines?

To condemn is easy, you said,
to condemn is to turn away

where no one will ever understand.
So, I go back, downtown,

to Jefferson Street, though
their haven, their Little Kitchen's gone.

I can cruise, can walk
and search each pane of glass

for that wave of heat,
the echo

that will fill the night
fifty years gone

206

when five men bent
in the diner's greasy light-

as Mongtomery darkened
beyond the window,

each bus offering its insult
or imagined slight-

and planned to kill a man
they'd never seen.

I can walk their streets,
though no one walks here anymore,

until I catch that curve
in a window or a windshield

that wrecks my face
so for a moment

I can mistake myself
for the redneck at the end of a joke.

Every map is open but a man,
and you can turn away

before you see how it's drawn,
or arrive too late

and miss that moment
when he sees himself as his language does,

when every other face
becomes the glass but his own.

Maybe the streetlamps remember the light,
gelid and thin as bacon fat,

as the vowel in your mouth
that just won't break,

a door I can walk through,
a room where I can sit beside them

hardly out of place,
then watch them rise and part

the city's yellow crepe of light,
and then a door I can open

to follow through the warehouse streets
to the city's fence

with a memory
only half my own.

I know these nights.
The sky is ash

and if you wait too long
your bones sing in your fingers,

cold as galvanized wire.
The rest of the way

comes from somewhere else.
There are many ways to get there

and then the one
I can't understand:

already,
maybe always being there.

Maybe they were born
into that vacant sky

and they were always there,
ready to force a choice

so they wouldn't have to
make one,

waiting for someone else
to write their names in air or water.

They never arrived,
so it didn't matter

they'd grabbed the wrong man,
wouldn't have mattered

if they'd found the one
they were looking for.

They'd still disappear,
like the bridge,

and be forgotten by the water.
They'd still come,

each one, to that morning
at the end of everything

when they'd look back
on the healing water

and say
My life hasn't meant a thing.

Some things are beyond us.

The moss never falls.
The river won't say a thing.

I lean, clouding
its reflected night.

And now I can't tell you
how I got here

or what I'd hoped to see,
what face would rise

if light swept from the channel
or the opposite shore.

The sky is empty,
and the river's bent

like a question too close
or too far away to read.

I don't do a lot of this versioning on paper. I usually work out syntax and the basic structure of the lines in a poem in my head, or in my throat, talking out the poem as I write it, so this is how these sentences were the first time I wrote them down. I played with the line breaks, which meant playing with the stanza shape as well- eventually settling on the short line, determined by the length of that first sentence. That becomes, to adopt a musical idea, the tonic everything else works from or toward.

But those first lines were written after much of the middle of the poem was written. I had some of the poem's images on paper and a few of the movements, but the poem wasn't in the right order; it wasn't moving properly. So, about a month or so after writing the phrases on the drafts I sent you, I started working on a new beginning—these lines—that gave the poem a pace, a line, a music that put everything in an order that worked.

This is pretty typical of my process: I spend some time writing notes, trying to get images or phrases on paper-to figure out what's going to go into the poem-without worrying about the order. After a fallow time, then I go back to those notes, this time trying to make the sentences. Or perhaps I should say the sentence, because I think of the poem as a single, long sentence that contains other sentences. It doesn't work until it has a rhythm, a significant rhythm, a gesture that everything carries. Much of the time I discover that rhythm by riffing, by talking the poem to the empty house, which worries the dog, or while I'm walking.

ACKNOWLEDGMENTS

"Americana Elegy" by Tommye Blount first appeared in *Fantasia for the Man in Blue* (Four Way Books, 2020).

"Applause" by Adrian C. Louis is from *Electric Snakes*, (University of Nebraska Press, 2018).

"Arrange Their Sea-Smooth Bones in Fourteen Broken Rows" by Steve Davenport *Uncontainable Noise* (Pavement Saw Press, 2006).

"Arrangements" by Ismael Angaluuk Hope first appeared in *Rock Piles Along the Eddy* by Ishmael Hope (Ishmael Reed Publications, 2017).

"Bag of Mice" by Nick Flynn first appeared in *Blind Huber* (Graywolf, 2002).

"Banned Portrait in the MAGA Era: Study Says Black Girls Are 'Less Innocent'" by Raina J. León first appeared in *black god mother this body* (Black Freighter Press, 2022).

"Bee Fennel" by Luke Johnson first appeared in *Porter Gulch Review*.

"Begin, Begin, Begin" by Jason Koo *No Rest* (Diode Editions, 2024).

"A Big Ball of foil in a Small NY Apartment" by Matthew Yeager first appeared in *NY Quarterly*; *Best American Poetry 2005*; *Like That* (Forklift Books, 2016).

"the black maria" by Aracelis Germay comes from *the black maria* (BOA, 2016).

"Borderless Bodies" by Linh Dinh first appeared in *Borderless Bodies* (Factory School, 2006).

"Camping Beneath the Dam" by CMarie Fuhrman first appeared in *Camping Beneath the Dam* (Etchings Press, 2020).

"Chimayó Milagros" by Sarah Rebecca Warren from *Arcturus*, fall 2017.

"Chiropractic (Bootblacks and Lightbulbs)" by Mark Wagenaar first appeared in *Subtropics*, Issue 11/12: winter/spring 2011.

"Corrosive Lyric" by Terry Hummer first appeared in *Skandalon*, (LSU Press, 2014).

"Cosmogony" by Ruth Ellen Kocher from *godhouse*, (Omnidawn, 2025).

"Creation Myth Number One" by Henry Israeli first appeared in *Praying to the Black Cat* (Del Sol, 2010).

"Curfew" by Brian Turner is from his *Here, Bullet* (Alice James Books, 2005).

"Darkly," is from Jake Adam York's *Murder Ballads* (Elixir Books, 2008).

"Deer on Crazy Creek" by Tami Haaland first appeared in *What Does Not Return* (Lost Horse Press, 2018).

"Digest of Red" by Linda Bryant Davis first appeared in *In the book Between Two Worlds* by Linda Bryant Davis (Act Power of Press, 2023).

"Distant Lover (Or, When You're Teaching In Amherst And, While On A Late Night Walk, Your Wife Calls From Brooklyn To Say Goodnight)" by John Murillo from *Kontemporary Amerikan Poetry* (Four Way Books, 2020).

"The Dragon" by Brigit Pegeen Kelly from *The Orchard*, (BOA Editions, 2004).

"Driving Through the Animal" by Enid Shomer, appeared in *Floodgate Poetry Series Vol. 3* (Upper Rubber Boot Books, November 2016).

"The Early Days of Aviation" by Connie Voisine first appeared in *Rare High Meadow of Which I Might Dream* (University of Chicago Press, 2008).

"Elemental" by Bill Brown comes from his book, Elemental, (3:A Taos Press, 2014).

"Fire Destroys Beloved Chicago Bakery" from *Scale*. Copyright © 2017 by Nathan McClain. Reprinted with the permission of The Permissions Company, LLC on behalf of Four Way Books, fourwaybooks.com.

"flight" by Lee Herrick first appeared in *Scar and Flower* (Word Poetry, 2018).

"Floaters" by Martín Espada first appeared in *Poetry* (November 2019) and then in his collection, *Floaters* (W.W. Norton, 2021). It is reprinted here with permission of the author.

"From Here to There" by Jeff Hardin first appeared in *Fall Sanctuary* (Storyline Press, 2005).

"Generation" by Suji Kwock Kim first appeared in *Esopus, Notes from the Divided Country* (LSU Press, 2003).

"Ghazal" from *Bring Now the Angels* by Dilruba Ahmed © 2020 reprinted by permission of the University of Pittsburgh Press, 2020. This poem also appeared in *Smartish Pace* (Issue 25, April 2018).

"A Good Education" by Juan J. Morales first appeared in *The Siren World* (Lithic Press, 2015).

"How to Live in the Burning World" by Deborah A. Miranda, *Altar for Broken Things* (BKMK Press, 2020).

"in my heart" by ire'ne lara silva is reprinted with permission from Saddle Road Press.

"Into the Valley Oak That Will Not Sing, That Will Not Even Talk" by J. Scott Brownlee first appeared in *The Adroit Journal*, Issue Thirteen (Fall 2015).

"The Last Days of Summer" by Gerard Robledo is from *My Mother, the Butcher*, Copyright © 2025 by Gerard Robledo. Reprinted with the permission of The Permissions Company, LLC on behalf of Texas Review Press, texasreviewpress.org.

"Last of December" by Todd Davis first appeared in *The Least of These* (Michigan State University Press, 2010).

"Leaving Saturn" by Major Jackson first appeared in *Leaving Saturn* (University of Georgia Press, 2002).

"A Love Poem" by Blas Falconer, apppeared in *Alaska Quarterly Review*, V34 no. 3/4, 2018. Also in *The Foundling Wheel*, (Four Way Books, 2012).

"Lucky" by Grant Clauser first appeared in *Reckless Constellations* (Cider Press, 2018).

"M16A2 Assault Rifle" by Hugh Martin first appeared in *Crazyhorse*, Issue Number 80, 2011. And *The Stick Soldiers* (BOA Editions, 2013).

"Machete," "Whiteface," and "Vallejo" from *Machete: Poems* by Tomás Q. Morín, copyright © 2021 by Tomás Q. Morín. Used by permission of Alfred A. Knopf, an imprint of the Knopf Doubleday Publishing Group, a division of Penguin Random House LLC. All rights reserved.

"Mad. Black. Bird." from *Ghost in a Black Girl's Throat* by Khalisa Rae, (Red Hen Press, 2021).

"Malouk's Qassida" by Khaled Mattawa first appeared in *New England Review*. 40. 65-66.

"Mama's Body" by Donovan McAbee from *Holy the Body*. Originally in *Trinity House Review #2*. Copyright © 2021 by Donovan McAbee. Reprinted with the permission of The Permissions Company, LLC on behalf of Texas Review Press, texasreviewpress.org.

"A Massive Dying Off" by Camille Dungy, *Smith Blue* (Southern Illinois University Press, 2011).

"Matthew 19:14" by Leah Silvieus from *Arabilis*, (Sundress Publications, 2019).

"Message from My Aunt on Her Son's Death Anniversary" by Zeina Hashem Beck first appeared in *Louder than Hearts* (Bauhan Publishing, 2017).

"Tatogana," from *Another Attempt at Rescue* by ML Smoker (Hanging Loose Press, 2005).

"Tattletale" by David Tomas Martinez first appeared in *Post Traumatic Hood Disorder* (Sarabande, 2019).

"Things to Tell My Son About the Moon" by Angela Narciso Torres first appeared in *Blood Orange* (Willow Books/Aquarius Press, 2013).

"This Stranger's Beauty" printed with the permission of Kimberly M. Blaeser and Holy Cow! Press.

"Times Like These: Marianna, Florida" by L. Lamar Wilson. *Callaloo*, vol. 33 no. 4, 2010, p. 1005-1005.

"To Fail and Fail and Still Go On" by Lauren Camp is from *An Eye in Each Square* (River River Books, 2023).

"Trying for Fire" by Tim Seibles first appeared in *Hurdy-Gurdy* (Cleveland State University Poetry Press, 1992).

"Two Video Installations" by Rick Barot first appeared in *Want* (Sarabande Books, 2008).

"Uncle" by Forrest Hamer first appeared in *Call & Response* (Alice James Books, 1995).

"Vestigia" by Aaron Coleman first appeared in *Threat Come Close* (Four Way Books, 2020).

"Water Tank Cosmogony" by Davis McCombs first appeared in *Dismal Rock* (Tupelo Press, 2007).

"Why Some Girls Love Horses" from *Animal Eye* by Paisley Rekdal © 2012. Reprinted by permission of the University of Pittsburgh Press.

"Winter After Strike" by Gregory Pardlo first appeared in *Ploughshares*, Spring 2002, 28:1. It was subsequently published in *Totem* by Gregory Pardlo, (American Poetry Review, 2007).

"Winter Cumbia with Brother and Sister" by Gustabo Hernandez first appeared on *The Night Heron Barks* (Spring 2020).

"The Winter's Wife" by Jennifer Chang previously appeared in *The New York Times*, *PBS NewsHour*, and *Some Say the Lark* (Alice James books, 2017).

"The World's Worst Jukebox" from *Imitation of Life*, by Allison Joseph (Carnegie Mellon UP, 2003).

ABOUT THE EDITOR

Andrew McFadyen-Ketchum founded PoemoftheWeek.com in 2006. He is author of *Fight or Flight*, *Visting Hours*, and *Ghost Gear*; acquisitions editor of Upper Rubber Boot Books; and editor and creator of *20 Years of PoemoftheWeek.com: 100 Poems by 100 Poets*, *The Floodgate Poetry Series*, and *Apocalypse Now: Poems and Prose from the End of Days.* In his free time he produces and hosts the *Nashville Poetry Party*—a little side project he started in 2024 that is slowly but surely taking over his life. Learn more at AndrewMK.com.

www.ingramcontent.com/pod-product-compliance
Lightning Source LLC
Chambersburg PA
CBHW031058020726
47495CB00007B/1949